SPOTLIGHT

# HONDURAS
# BAY ISLANDS

## CHRIS HUMPHREY & AMY E. ROBERTSON

D0878952

# Contents

# HONDURAS
# BAY ISLANDS

# THE BAY ISLANDS

The white powdery sand, transparent waters, and abundant sea life of these emerald islands and their coral cays form Honduras's most popular attraction. As one of the world's cheapest places for scuba certification, the Bay Islands (Islas de la Bahía) are a paradise for novice and experienced divers alike, while snorkelers can simply wade out a few feet to immerse themselves in the rich undersea world boasting hundreds of multihued species of fish and coral.

For novice scuba divers, finding a more convenient place to get an Open Water certification or advanced training would be difficult. Eager instructors by the dozen are just waiting around for their next client, ready to take potential divers through the paces in calm, clear, 28°C (82°F) waters, all at remarkably low prices.

Diving and snorkeling may be the activities of choice for many Bay Island visitors, but life above the waves has its own appeal. The islands have a tangled history of pirate raids, immigration, deportation, and conquest, including more than 200 years of British ownership of Roatán, Utila, and Guanaja. English is the first language of most native islanders, some settlers from the British Cayman Islands, others Black Caribs that claim runaway slaves as ancestors—although recent influxes of mainlanders ("the Spanish," as the islanders like to say) are spreading the use of the Spanish language. Resident expatriates have opened restaurants that span global cuisine, but seafood is naturally the traditional culinary choice, and grilled lobster dinners can be found for as little as 10 dollars.

© AMY E. ROBERTSON

# HIGHLIGHTS

◖ **Diving Roatán's Reef:** Diving around all three Bay Islands is spectacular, and there are 100 dive sites surrounding Roatán alone, including walls and channels, sunken shipwrecks, and caverns. Hawksbill turtles, moray eels, spotted eagle rays, and yellowtail damselfish are just a few of the species easily spotted among the colorful coral gardens (page 22).

◖ **Fishing:** The waters off Roatán, with shallow, sandy waters on the south side and a 3,000-meter-deep channel on the north, are perfectly situated for fishing excursions in pursuit of marlin, wahoo, tarpon, barracuda, kingfish, and more (page 23).

◖ **West Bay:** Roatán's West Bay is a vision of Caribbean bliss, a powdery ribbon of white sand in front of sparkling clear turquoise water with coral reef just steps offshore (page 35).

◖ **Utila's Nightlife:** Those after the international traveler party life will not want to miss a few days frequenting the many bars making up the nightlife on Utila (page 65).

◖ **Utila Cays:** With their crystal waters and powdery, isolated beaches, the tiny cays off the island of Utila make for getaways that are fantasies come true. What might seem like the realm of millionaires – the rental of an entire island – is available on Sandy Cay or Little Cay for just US$100-115 a night, while budget travelers can pop over to islets like Water Cay for a secluded picnic or campout (page 77).

◖ **Guanaja's North-Side Beaches:** These rarely visited beaches, like Dina Beach and West End, are home to nothing but kilometers of sand and palm trees, where you can camp or stay in one of the low-key and reasonably priced hotels (page 81).

◖ **Chachahuate:** Long popular as a day trip from either Roatán or the mainland's north coast, newly developed cabin rentals and even a small hotel now make the Garífuna village of Chachahuate in the Cayos Cochinos a fantastic place to spend a few days snorkeling and sunning, at a fraction of the cost of the other Bay Islands (page 87).

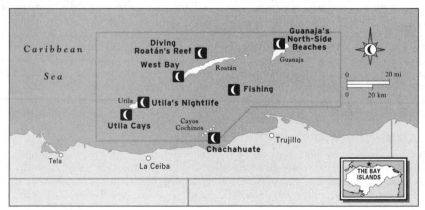

LOOK FOR ◖ TO FIND RECOMMENDED SIGHTS, ACTIVITIES, DINING, AND LODGING.

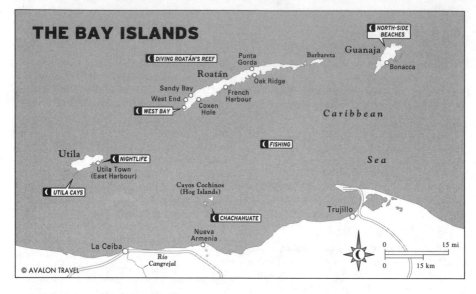

High season for Bay Islands tourism is most of the year apart from the September–November hurricane season. Vacation times in Central America, such as Christmas, Easter week, and the first two weeks in August, can be very hard times to find lodging, especially on Roatán, and many establishments take advantage to jack up their prices. Mid-January to mid-February is a great time to come to the islands, as tourists are fewer. September is the best month to take advantage of the low season prices, as it tends to be less rainy than October and November.

## PLANNING YOUR TIME

You can never have too much time on the islands, a fact the many expatriates living there will cheerfully confirm. But most of us are on a tighter schedule. If you have only a few days or a week on the Bay Islands, you'll probably end up choosing between the three. Which island to visit is really a question of personal taste. All are surrounded by coral reef. Roatán is by far the most popular, with plenty of great beaches, towns, services like hotels, restaurants and dive shops, and places to explore to keep divers and nondivers alike happy for a week or

more. Utila is smaller, with only one town and a couple of beaches, and is generally more popular with those focused on diving and the low-budget international traveler crowd. Nondivers will likely only want to spend a couple of days here. Guanaja is much less frequently visited than the other two, but it has equally good reef, a few hotels and dive resorts, and many deserted beaches to wander. Divers may want to stay a week, but nondivers again will likely feel content with a few days for R&R.

Those planning on doing some serious diving or taking a four-day scuba certification course will plan on five days or a week, with all the amazing diving on offer. A week or more would allow for trips out to more far-flung dive sites, which are often in the best condition. Many of the dive resorts on the islands specialize in weeklong dive, room, and meal packages, often around US$1,000–1,800 per person.

All three of the main Bay Islands are serviced by air flights Monday–Saturday, and Roatán has flights on Sunday as well. Utila and Roatán also have daily ferries to and from La Ceiba, and ferry service from Trujillo to Guanaja is available twice a week. There are a few charter air and boat services as well. Both air and ferry service can be suspended in the event of bad weather. October and November are the rainiest months, while high season is mid-December through May (although there can still be frequent rain in December and early January). September can be a great time to visit, taking advantage of low-season rates, but typically enjoying good weather.

## THE LAND

The Bay Islands, arrayed in an arc between 29 and 56 kilometers off the Caribbean coast of Honduras, are the above-water expression of the Bonacca Ridge, an extension of the mainland Sierra de Omoa mountain range that disappears into the ocean near Puerto Cortés. The Bonacca Ridge forms the edge of the Honduran continental shelf in the Caribbean. Thus, on the northern, ocean-facing side of the three main islands, shallow waters extend only just beyond the shore before disappearing over sheer underwater cliffs to the deep waters, while on the south side the waters fronting the Honduran mainland are much shallower. The height of the islands generally increases west to east, from the lowland swamps of Utila to the modest mid-island ridges of Roatán to two noteworthy peaks on Guanaja, the highest being 412 meters.

### Flora and Fauna

Ecological zones in the Bay Islands include pine and oak savannah, arid tropical forest, beach vegetation, mangrove swamp, and iron shore, or fossilized, uplifted coral. Much of the once-dense native pine and oak forests has not survived centuries of sailors seeking masts, immigrants looking for building material, and hunters setting fires to scare game. The only forests left are on the privately owned island of Barbareta and in a few remote sections of Roatán, like by Brick Bay or around Port Royal. What was left of the famed forests of Guanaja was utterly flattened by Hurricane Mitch's 290-kph winds—the island's vegetation has only recently begun to recover.

Many of the once-abundant animal species endemic to the Bay Islands have been hunted to extinction or to the brink of it: Manatees, seals, fresh- and saltwater turtles, white-tailed deer, green iguanas, basilisk lizards, boa constrictors, yellow-crowned and red-lored Amazon parrots, frigate birds, brown pelicans, and roseate terns have all vanished or are now seen only rarely. Crocodiles were once frequently seen crossing streets in Utila, but when one was spotted (and promptly killed) in December 1995, the event was a major local news item.

In spite of the depredations of hunters, 15 species of lizard still survive on the islands, along with 13 species of snake (including the poisonous but rarely seen coral), wild pigs, the small rat-like agouti, two species of opossum, and 13 species of bat. More than 120 bird species, most of which are migratory, have been spotted on the islands. Once at least 27 species of macaws, parrots, and parakeets lived on the islands; now the only macaws found are pets, and only about half the parrot species still survive in the wild.

The Bay Islands Conservation Association (BICA, www.bicautila.org), with offices on all three islands, coordinates efforts to protect different endangered species as well as the islands' remaining forests by overseeing reserves at Port Royal and Carambola in Roatán, Turtle Harbour in Utila, and, supposedly, the entire island of Guanaja. BICA now also oversees the entire reef around Utila with a marine patrol, except for the shallow waters around the cays, from which only the fishermen of the cays can fish. They've also been active in Utila distributing environmentally friendly bug spray, doing bird surveys, and conducting ecotours.

### Climate

The Bay Islands have a superbly comfortable climate, with year-round air temperatures ranging 25–29°C (77–84°F) and east–southeast trade winds blowing steadily most of the year. Temperatures average 27°C (81°F) in the daytime, 21°C (70°F) at night—hot but not stifling during the day, and pleasant for sleeping at night.

Annual rainfall averages 220 centimeters,

## COPING WITH THE INSECTS

Sand flies and mosquitoes can be voracious on the Bay Islands, so come prepared. Sand flies (also called jejenes and "no-see-ums") can be a nightmare on the beach, turning the arms and legs of an unsuspecting sunbather into pincushions of little red welts. Avon Skin-So-Soft and coconut oil are good repellents, as, of course, are long, loose-fitting clothes. DEET works great, but kills the coral, so be sure to rinse off before heading into the water. A good stiff breeze will get rid of the sand flies entirely, so with luck, the trade winds will be blowing during your trip. Some beaches, including Roatán's famed West Bay Beach, are sprayed with eco-friendly insecticides, which has been highly effective in eliminating the problem.

more than half of this coming in October and November, the height of the hurricane season. Water visibility is best when there is the least rain, usually March–September. Water temperature ranges from 26°C (79°F) midwinter to 30°C (86°F) in summer. The rains usually start in summer, often in June, and continue until December or January. February and March are usually the driest months. However, weather patterns vary widely from year to year, and rain can hit at any time.

# HISTORY
## Pre-Columbian Residents

In spite of almost 50 identified archaeological sites, little is known of the early inhabitants of the Bay Islands. Most archaeologists now agree, after years of dispute, that pre-Columbian islanders were related to the mainland Pech, who, prior to conquest, lived close to the coast near Trujillo. These island Amerindians are sometimes referred to as "Paya," but that is a term that has been rejected by the Pech, as it was a demeaning word used by the Spanish conquerors to mean wild or savage.

The first full-time residents are thought to have arrived no earlier than A.D. 600. After A.D. 1000, several major residential areas sprang up, such as Plan Grande in eastern Guanaja and the "80-Acre" site in eastern Utila. Because all the sites are located inland 10–20 meters above sea level, one theory has it that the first islanders hated sand flies even more than the current residents and fled the shoreline to escape the pests.

The island Pech grew manioc (cassava) and corn, hunted for deer and other game, fished from dugout canoes for reef fish and shark, and carried on a lively trade with the mainland Maya and Pech, as evidenced by discoveries of obsidian, flint, and ceramics with mainland designs.

Most pre-Columbian sites have long since been thoroughly sacked by fortune hunters both foreign and local. The best place to see examples of pottery and jade is in the museum at Anthony's Key Resort in Sandy Bay, Roatán. Locals may still try to sell visitors "yaba-ding-dings," as they call the artifacts, but after years of looting there aren't many pieces left to sell.

## Conquest and Colonization

Believed to be the first European to visit the Bay Islands, Columbus landed near Soldado Beach on Guanaja in late July 1502 on his fourth voyage. After anchoring and sending his brother Bartholomew ashore for a look around, the admiral named the island "Isla de los Pinos" (Island of the Pines) in honor of the impressive forests. He then commandeered a passing merchant canoe laden with goods from the mainland and forced its owner to accompany him to the Mosquitia coast to serve as an interpreter. He remarked in his journal on a "very robust people who adore idols and live mostly from a certain white grain with which they make fine bread and the most perfect beer."

When the Spaniards returned on a slaving expedition in 1516, they made off with 300 Indians after a brief skirmish, only to have the would-be slaves take over the ship near Cuba and promptly set sail back to their home. But other ships looking for slaves soon followed, and not long after that, in 1530, the first *encomienda* was awarded on the Bay Islands. *Encomiendas* granted a conquistador rights to demand labor and tribute from the local inhabitants, theoretically in return for good governance and religious education.

This new economy had barely been established when European freebooters began appearing on the horizon, drooling at the thought of all the gold mined in the interior of Honduras passing through relatively isolated and unprotected Trujillo. French raiding boats appeared in 1536, followed by the English, who used the Bay Islands as a hideout for the first confirmed time in 1564, after capturing four Spanish frigates.

By the early 17th century, the persistent use of the Bay Islands as a base for pirate assaults and, briefly, as a settlement area for the British Providence Company had become a serious threat to the Spanish, so colonial authorities decided to depopulate the islands. By 1650 all the native islanders had been removed, most with the sorry fate of ending up in the malarial lowlands on Guatemala's Caribbean coast. The now-uninhabited islands were even more appealing to the pirates, who pursued their ventures unabated.

The many pirates who found shelter on the islands before the British military occupation in 1742—including Henry Morgan, John Coxen, John Morris, Edward Mansfield, and a host of others—spent most of their time hunting, fishing, or fixing up their boats, never bothering to set up any buildings beyond temporary camps. Smaller groups preferred to anchor in the bay on the south side of Guanaja, with at least seven escape routes through the cays and reef, while larger fleets stayed at Port Royal, Roatán, with just one narrow, easily defensible entrance.

Following the declaration of war between England and Spain in 1739, British troops occupied Port Royal for several years, building two small forts and granting homesteads in Port Royal and Sandy Bay. The Spanish were awarded the islands as part of the Treaty of Aix-la-Chapelle in 1748, and the last settlers were finally removed in 1751. The British returned in 1779 following another outbreak of war. In 1782 Spaniards attacked Port Royal with 12 ships and took the forts after two days of fierce fighting. The forts and surrounding town were destroyed, and Roatán was left uninhabited.

## Development of the Modern Bay Islands

The earliest immigrant settlement in the Bay Islands that has survived to the present day is the Garífuna village at Punta Gorda, Roatán. Some 4,000 Garífuna were unceremoniously dumped on the deserted island on April 12, 1797, by the British near Port Royal. Most of the Garífuna moved on to the mainland shortly thereafter, settling first at Trujillo and then elsewhere up and down the coast, but one group decided they liked the looks of Roatán and settled at Punta Gorda.

The Garífuna were followed in the 1830s by a wave of immigrants, both white and black, leaving the Cayman Islands in the wake of the abolition of slavery there. Although some isolated settlers lived on the islands when the Cayman Islanders arrived, the newcomers laid the foundations for the present-day towns. They moved first to Suc-Suc (Pigeon) Cay off Utila in 1831, and shortly thereafter to Coxen Hole, Flowers Bay, and West End in Roatán and Sheen and Hog Cays off Guanaja, which would eventually become Bonacca Town.

The British government, seeing the Bay Islands as a useful geopolitical tool in its struggle with the United States for control over Central America, initially claimed ownership of the islands. In 1859, the British were forced to recognize Honduran sovereignty over the Bay Islands, but many islanders continued to think they were part of the British empire until the early 20th century, when the Honduran government first began asserting its authority over the islands.

## Current Society

The economy of the Bay Islands has long relied almost entirely on the ocean, despite brief forays into the banana and pineapple exportation business in the late 19th century. Fishing has always been and continues to be the mainstay of the economy, with a fleet of some 400 commercial boats on all three islands, fishing mainly for shrimp, lobster, and conch. Overfishing has led to bans *(vedas)* during certain months of the year, but with only two inspectors, the several plants on Roatán pretty much buy whatever comes their way, whatever time of year it is. A modest boat-building industry, based particularly in Oak Ridge, has declined in recent years. Islander men frequently join on with the merchant marine or work on international cruise ships for several months of the year.

This low-key existence began to change starting in the late 1960s, when tourists discovered the islands' reefs, beaches, and funky culture. Since the late 1980s, the pace has picked up dramatically. In 1990, an estimated 15,000 tourists came to the islands; by 1996 it was 60,000. The accelerating development of Bay Island tourism took a blow from Hurricane Mitch in 1998 and the ensuing bad publicity. But as memories of the hurricane have faded (at least outside Honduras), tourists are returning to the islands in skyrocketing numbers, and further growth and development is underway. The cruise ship trade is also accelerating, with anywhere from one to eight ships a week docking at Roatán, depending on the season, unloading 250,000–300,000 cruise shippers a year. (That's roughly one-third of all tourists to Honduras.) Carnival Cruise Lines is building a second ship terminal to accommodate the dramatic growth, scheduled to open in the fall of 2009.

The changes wrought by tourism have benefited many islanders immensely, and most now live off the trade in one way or another. Even before the tourist boom, islanders had always maintained a better standard of living than their mainland countrymen. Consequently, a steadily growing number of Latino immigrants have come over to get a piece of the good life, and foreigners (particularly Canadians and Americans) continue to come in increasing numbers to run a business or to retire—trends some islanders are not too happy about. The last census put the population of all three islands at about 38,000, with an annual growth rate of 9 percent (compared to just under 3 percent for the country as a whole).

# Scuba Diving

Upon arrival in the Bay Islands, divers can be overwhelmed by the number of dive shops and courses. Here's some basic information to get you started, whether you're a first-time diver in need of certification or an old hand looking for the right shop.

## GETTING CERTIFIED

First, try to realistically decide if you are ready to go diving. Bay Islands dive instructors have many stories of would-be students who, believe it or not, could barely swim or were actually scared of the water. Although it's relatively cheap and other people seem to like it, if you just can't get rid of that lurking panic after a couple of shallow dives, accept the fact that diving is not for you. One of the best ways to find out how you will react to scuba diving is to try snorkeling a few times to see how you feel in the underwater world. Some people find they prefer the more relaxed shallow-water experience of snorkeling, which does not require all the gear, training, and expense of scuba diving.

Most divers getting certified in the Bay Islands follow a course created by the Professional Association of Dive Instructors (PADI), the best-known scuba certification organization. Almost all dive shops on the islands work with PADI, but a couple of shops have other certifications instead or as well, such as Scuba Schools International (SSI) and National

# COURSE AND DIVE PRICES

Below are the standard course and dive prices, but naturally they are subject to change. While Utila used to be significantly less expensive than Roatán, that's no longer such a big factor, especially for dive courses. When budgeting, remember that courses on Utila include hostel-style accommodations if desired, and that the required accompanying dive book can run US$30 and up, depending on the course. Prices outside of West End in Roatán can be a bit higher.

- **Open Water:** US$250-325 (Roatán), US$270 (Utila)

- **Advanced Open Water:** US$250-300 (Roatán), US$270 (Utila)

- **Rescue:** US$250 (Roatán), US$270 (Utila)

- **Dive Master:** US$670-770 (Roatán), US$750-835 (Utila) – these prices include the US$70 PADI fee

- **Single Dive:** US$35 (Roatán), US$35 or two for US$55 (Utila)

- **Ten-Dive Package:** US$250-300 (Roatán), US$220-250 (Utila)

The Open Water certificate at Coral Bay Resort on Guanaja costs US$375.

Association of Underwater Instructors (NAUI). While PADI is by far the most popular, all three organizations have good reputations, and almost all scuba shops around the world accept certifications from any of them.

Novices ready to take the plunge into the world of scuba have a choice of either a Discover Scuba Diving or Open Water certification. A **Discover Scuba Diving** course, normally costing US$70–125 (with the cheaper rates at Utila dive shops), is an introductory dive for those who aren't sure if they'll like diving or not. It involves a half day of instruction followed by a shallow, controlled dive.

The **Open Water certification** is typically 3.5–4 days, starting with half a day of videos, then a couple of days combining classroom work, shallow water dives, and open-water dives. The last day is two open-water dives. You are then allowed to dive without an instructor—but never without another diver, invariably a dive master. It's standard practice in the Bay Islands for all divers to go out with a dive master or instructor, as guides and to ensure the protection of the reef.

Dive shops will sometimes take referrals, wherein a person completes the academic and shallow-water training at home and finishes the open-water dives with the shop. Considering that the shallow-water training could be accomplished for less money in balmy, clear Caribbean waters instead of the local YMCA pool, there's not much attraction in using a referral unless your time on the islands is extremely limited.

Many newly certified divers come out of their Open Water course feeling slightly uneasy about the idea of diving without a reassuring veteran instructor at their shoulder; they may want to immediately continue their controlled training with the **Advanced Open Water course.** The advanced course offers five different advanced dive options, with two required: instruction in undersea navigation and multilevel diving—essential for planning your own dives—and a deep dive (to 30 meters). Other dive choices include multilevel, night, wrecks, naturalist, photography, search and recover, and peak performance buoyancy. Some shops will combine two of these in one dive (for example, photography and naturalist).

Recreational divers are allowed to descend to a maximum depth of 30 meters. Going deeper puts divers in serious danger of both nitrogen narcosis and severe decompression problems when ascending. With a different mix of gases in the air tanks, however, it is possible with training to descend deeper and stay down longer than with a regular air tank. Nitrox, a mix of nitrogen and oxygen, allows divers to (depending on the mix) extend their time at depth by 20 or 30 minutes or minimize the surface

# THE BAY ISLANDS REEF SYSTEM

Coral reefs are one of the most complex ecosystems on the planet, comparable in diversity to tropical rainforests. The Bay Islands reef is particularly varied because of its location on the edge of the continental shelf, at the transition between shallow-water and deep-water habitats. Some 96 percent of all species of marine life known to inhabit the Caribbean – from tiny specks of glowing bioluminescence to the whale shark, the largest fish in the world – have been identified in the waters surrounding the Bay Islands. Divers and snorkelers flock here in droves to experience a dizzying assortment of fishes, sponges, anemones, worms, shellfish, rays, sea turtles, sharks, dolphins, and hard and soft corals.

## WHAT IS CORAL?

Contrary to what many people understandably assume, coral is a stationary animal, not a plant. Each "branch" of coral is made up of hundreds or thousands of tiny flowerlike polyps. Polyps, thin-membraned invertebrates, compensate for their flimsy bodies by extracting calcium carbonate from the seawater and converting it into a brittle limestone skeleton. Through this continual, tireless construction process, the bizarre and beautiful undersea forests seen by divers and snorkelers are created, at a rate of about a centimeter per year.

Tiny, extended tentacles bring in food drifting by in the water, but the anchored coral polyps must supplement their intake by housing minuscule algae cells; these cells in turn produce nutrients for the polyps through photosynthesis. Because of this symbiotic relationship, coral always grows in relatively shallow waters, where the sun can penetrate. Reduced water clarity due to pollution or erosion from construction, agriculture, or deforestation can be fatal for coral, robbing the algae of the light needed to photosynthesize.

The main reef-building coral in shallow areas is leafy lettuce coral *(Agaricia tenuifolia)*. This species virtually excludes other corals from many spur tops, growing in some areas to within 10 centimeters of the surface. In areas with greater wave energy, such as along the north sides of the islands, forests of treelike elkhorn coral *(Acropora palmata)* are common. Star coral *(Montastrea annularis)*, brain coral *(Diploria spp.)*, boulder brain coral *(Colpophylia natans)*, and elegant columns of pillar coral *(Dendrogyra cylindrus)* are often seen on the fore reef, at a depth of 10–15 meters. Black coral is still found around the Bay Islands, usually in deeper waters on reef walls. Many shallower patches have been destroyed by jewelry-makers. In the water, black coral appears silver, only turning black when exposed to the air.

**Fire coral,** or hydrocoral, is not a true coral but a "battery of stinging nematocysts on tentacles of coral polyps," as Paul Humann, author of a good three-volume reference on reef systems, describes it. Learn what fire coral looks like right away, and keep well clear of it – even a light brush can be painful. Should you accidentally bump into it, remember never to rub the affected area or wash it with fresh water or soap, as this can cause untriggered nematocysts to release their barbs. Two recommended treatments are vinegar or meat tenderizer, both of which immobilize the nematocysts.

## THE REEF

It's often claimed that the Bay Islands reef and the Belize reef system to the north together make up the second-longest reef in the world – after Australia's Great Barrier Reef. Technically, the Bay Islands reef is distinct from the Belize reef – not only does a 3,000-meter-deep undersea trench separate the two, but they are different kinds of reef. The Belize system is a barrier reef, with the coral wall separated from shore by a lagoon at least a mile wide, while the Bay Islands system is a fringing reef, essentially beginning right from the shore. Sections of the north-side reef on the Bay Islands show characteristics of developing into a barrier reef in time but are still considered fringing reef.

Reef geography is generally the same on all three of the main islands. The north-side reef forms almost a complete wall, with only a few narrow passages allowing access to the shallow lagoon between the reef and the shore. The

Guanaja north-side reef is much farther off-shore (about a mile, or 1.5 kilometers, in places) than on Utila and Roatán. From the reef crest, which sometimes almost breaks the surface, the reef slopes to a plateau at around 10 meters, then falls off the wall. The south-side reef frequently starts literally at the water's edge and slopes down at a more gentle grade to a depth of around 10-12 meters, when it hits the sheer reef wall bottoming on sand at around 30-40 meters. The southern reef is generally more broken up than the north, with channels, chutes, headlands, and cays. Sea mounts – hills of coral rising up off the ocean floor – and spur-and-groove coral ridges are common and are often the best places to see diverse sea life.

The Cayos Cochinos reef system shares similar characteristics with the other islands, except it lacks steep drop-offs and lagoons on the north side.

## THE HEALTH OF THE REEF

Generally speaking, the Bay Islands reef is in pretty good shape, although certain high-impact areas are showing signs of damage from overdiving and decreasing water quality. According to a recent study, the Roatán reef has 25-30 percent live coral cover (the rest covered by sand, sea grass, sponges, rubble, algae, dead coral, fire coral, etc.), a relatively healthy percentage compared to other Caribbean reefs.

Tourism development poses the most direct threat to the reef, since coastal and hillside construction generates runoff and other forms of water pollution. Degraded water quality leads to algae blooms, which steal sunlight, oxygen, and other nutrients from the coral, literally choking the reef to death. This threat is particularly severe on Roatán, where the island's long central ridge is being carved up on all sides for roads and houses, while coastal wetlands, which filter runoff, are being filled in for construction. The reef off West Bay in Roatán is particularly threatened, due to all the construction and tourist activity in the hills backing the beach. While Guanaja is quite hilly, construction on the main island is still limited, making runoff less serious. However, water pollution around Bonacca, Mangrove Bight, and Savanna Bight has damaged most of the reef surrounding those towns. Utila, mostly flat and still retaining much of its wetlands, does not face much erosion at the moment, but water pollution is a problem around East Harbour and Pigeon Cay.

Coral bleaching occurs on the Bay Islands reef, as it does on reefs all over the world. During these usually temporary events, higher water temperatures than normal cause the coral to expel the zooxanthellae (algae cells) that give coral its color pigments. The cells return when the sea temperature returns to its normal level, ideally 23-30°C (73-86°F). In 1998-1999, there was a global bleaching event, in part as a result of the warming of the world's seas after the 1997-1998 El Niño phenomenon. Hurricane Mitch – so devastating above the water – helped spur the recovery of the Bay Islands reef from the prolonged bleaching episode by bringing up colder water from deeper in the ocean and cooling off the waters near the surface by as much as 3°C.

The proliferation of divers is beginning to take a toll on the reef; some oversaturated dive sites are closed off to allow for the coral to recover. These days, dive boats more regularly tie off on buoys instead of anchoring on the reef, but divers continue to bump and grab coral in spite of frequent warnings. Each brush with a piece of coral wipes off a defensive film covering the polyps, allowing bacteria to penetrate. Just one small gap can compromise the defenses of an entire coral colony. Think about that when you see the reef in front of West Bay Beach, Roatán, swarmed with thousands of cruise-ship visitors.

Black coral, formerly common around the Bay Islands, has been depleted in recent years by jewelry-makers, whose work can be seen in several local gift shops. For those tempted to buy a piece, remember it is illegal to take black coral into the United States.

Two websites with detailed research information on the Bay Island reef system are www.yale.edu/roatan/index.htm and www.wfu.edu/~dkevans.

## DIVING SAFETY

Fortunately, safety standards are high throughout the Bay Islands. But when choosing your shop, it is a good idea to personally verify minimal safety standards. Below is a set of questions to ask (and be sure to verify the answers with your own eyes; don't just take the staff's word for it).

- Do you carry oxygen on the boat?

- Do you carry a VHF radio? (A cell phone is not nearly as reliable.)

- Does the boat stay at the dive site after dropping off divers?

- Is the boat manned by a captain at all times? (Some shops expect dive masters or instructors to also serve as the captain.)

- When was your air last analyzed? (The analysis certificate should be dated within the past three months.)

interval and allow more dives in a single day. As well, divers seem to be slightly less tired at the end of the day. Nitrox is very popular with live-aboard dive boats, which try to squeeze in as many dives as possible in a week. Nitrox diving requires certification and special equipment, which not every dive shop has. Extreme depth freaks will be pleased to hear that another, even more specialized gas mix known as Trimix (Nitrox plus helium) allows divers to go as deep as 150 meters, a truly spooky deep-sea world.

Nitrox has become pretty widely available, but Trimix is less common, and easier to find on Utila. The Bay Islands College of Diving and Utila Dive Center offer full tech courses, Trimix, and rebreathers. Ocean Connections in West End has one complete Trimix set.

## CHOOSING A SHOP

So, you've decided you're ready to take a course or go on a series of dives. How to choose between all the different dive shops? Both Utila and Roatán have set minimum prices among nearly all of their shops to avoid price wars—that price is currently at US$250 for an Open Water course in Utila and US$280 for an Open Water course in West End, Roatán. A few shops charge more, but typically include course materials and other fees (Utila has a US$4 daily reef tax, and Roatán a once-annually US$10 Marine Park fee). Dive shops do get together throughout the year, though, to change prices based on the cost of fuel and the level of activity on the islands, so these prices may fluctuate. Guanaja has fewer dive shops, and they are more expensive.

Perhaps the most important criteria for choosing a shop, especially for novice divers taking their first course, is the quality of the instructors. A good instructor can mean the difference between a fun, safe, and informative course, and one that just follows the book—or worse. Certified divers will also want to ensure their dive leader is competent, as they will be, in part, relying on that person's judgment and safety skills. Ask how many dives a dive master has completed—100 is very few; 500 is a decent amount; 1,000 or more is a lot. Also, a dive master with 100 or so dives is likely to have gone through all or most of his or her courses on the Bay Islands, where conditions are excellent much of the time. Consequently, that dive master will have less experience dealing with emergency situations than a diver trained in, for instance, the North Sea or the northern Pacific off California. At the same time, experience on Bay Island reefs is essential to understanding local conditions. If you can find an instructor who has worked on the islands for several years but also has experience in other parts of the world, that's best of all. Dive masters trained in commercial diving, mixed-gas diving, cave diving, or military diving can be very good because of their experience, but they are also sometimes extremely cavalier with safety precautions.

After talking to the dive masters, look closely at the gear you would be using. The newer, the better. Especially crucial is having a well-maintained air compressor to ensure clean air in your tank. Cast an eye over the hoses, regulator, and BCD air vest, which should all look new and be without signs of wear and tear. Most shops should and do replace their gear on a regular basis. Ensure fins and mask fit snugly and comfortably—this may seem like a trivial detail in the dive shop, but a tight fin or a leaky mask can be very distracting in the water and ruin a dive if annoying enough. A large dive boat is also a great bonus, much more stable and easier to get in and out of than the smaller launches used by many shops, and provides a less choppy and wet ride to and from the dive sites—but it usually also means more divers at each site. Those prone to seasickness should bring motion sickness pills, which are sold by many dive shops. Waters around the Bay Islands are usually a fairly balmy 28°C (82°F) or so, but if the water temperatures get down to the low 20s, as they sometimes do, you will want to make sure your shop has good wetsuits, full-length if you get cold easily.

Another factor to consider is the setup and schedule of dives at the different shops. Utila shops usually send out two dive boats a day for a total of four dives, two on the morning boat (around 7 A.M.) and another two on the afternoon boat (around 1 P.M.). Roatán shops usually send out three dive boats a day with one dive each, at 9 A.M., 11 A.M., and 2 P.M., although some have dives half an hour earlier or later. While the shop chooses the sites, clients should not be shy in requesting certain dives. Most dive shops are happy to accommodate, although some may put up resistance in going to a far-off site. And be sure the group you are going with will not be too large. An ideal group size is 4–6 divers, dive master included. Certainly, you don't want to go with more than eight divers, or it starts to feel a bit like an underwater procession. Be aware that many shops advertise low instructor-to-student or dive master-to-diver ratios, but fail to mention that their groups number 12 or 15 divers, with three or four dive masters/instructors to herd everybody along.

# Roatán

*Rattan-Island is about 30 miles long and 13 broad, about eight leagues distant from the coast of Honduras.... The south side is very convenient for shipping, having many fine harbours. The north side is defended by a reef of rocks that extend from one end of the island to the other, having but few passages through, and those of but small note, being mostly made use of by the turtlers.... It is likewise very healthy, the inhabitants hereabouts generally living to a great age.*

*– Thomas Jefferys, Geographer to the King of England, 1762*

Jefferys may have been a bit off on the measurements—Roatán is actually about 40 miles (64 kilometers) long and only a little over 2 miles (3.2 kilometers) wide—but he did accurately describe the natural features that have long made Roatán the choice of Bay Island immigrants, from the first pirates 400 years ago to the resort builders, vacationers, and expatriates of today.

Tourists and retirees began arriving on Roatán in the 1960s, and in recent years the influx has increased dramatically. Roatán has been deemed respectable—enjoying fawning write-ups in travel publications and the limelight of frequent celebrity sightings—and is now home to a large expatriate community consisting mainly of Americans but also many Canadians and a sprinkling of Europeans.

After years of raging real-estate speculation and building fever, few nooks and crannies have escaped the scrutiny of developers. Remote sections of coastline on all sides of the island have been divided up in lots for development as private homes or resorts. Nevertheless, towns like

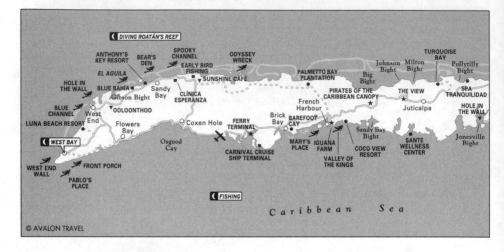

West End and Sandy Bay remain relatively slow-paced and not outrageously expensive when compared to other Caribbean islands.

One facet of the tourist profile that sets Roatán apart from the other Bay Islands is the international cruise ships. The monstrous crafts come in several days a week, especially in high season, and disgorge hundreds of tourists for the day. West Bay can get rather crowded those days, particularly at the southern end of the beach. While the crowds can be a bit disconcerting for other foreign visitors, the islanders are all for the new business, especially since the tourists spend well and only stay for the day, thus offering high income and limited stress on local infrastructure.

Theories on the source of the island's name vary wildly. The most popular explanation, supported by Jefferys and many other colonial-era chroniclers, is that Roatán is a derivation of rattan, the English word for a common vine found in the Caribbean. Another possibility is that it's a severe corruption of the Nahuatl expression *coatl-tlan,* "place of women." A third, far-fetched hypothesis is that the name comes from the English expression "Rat-land," referring to the island's pirate inhabitants.

Just less than two-thirds of the Bay Islands' population, or around 22,000 people, live on Roatán. Coxen Hole, the island's largest town,

is the department capital. Thanks to highly effective spraying, sand flies are no longer the plague they once were on Roatán, although it's always wise to pack repellent.

## GETTING THERE
### Air

As the most frequently visited of the three Bay Islands, Roatán has plenty of air service, although much of it comes via La Ceiba. There are also a few direct flights per week to the United States, and for those staying at one of the Henry Morgan resorts, weekly charter flights from Milan, Rome, and Toronto. Those flying out of Roatán to an international destination must pay a US$34 departure tax in the Roatán airport; for a domestic flight the departure tax is US$2.

**Sosa** (tel. 504/445-1154) offers flights twice daily to and from La Ceiba (US$56), with connections to San Pedro Sula, Tegucigalpa, and the Mosquitia. **Taca/Isleña** (tel. 504/445-1918, www.taca.com, www.flyislena.com) offers twice-daily flights to San Pedro Sula and thrice-daily flights to La Ceiba with connections onward to Tegucigalpa and elsewhere, including Miami, New York, and Houston.

At the time of writing, **Continental** (no office in Roatán, www.continental.com) was running two flights on Saturday and one each

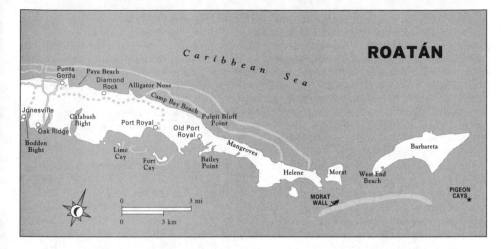

on Sunday and Wednesday direct between Roatán and Houston, Texas, a less than three-hour trip.

**Delta** (www.delta.com) also has two direct flights to Roatán from Atlanta on Saturdays, with service to San Pedro Sula (3–4 flights per week) and Tegucigalpa (4–5 flights per week).

There are a couple of charter services available for local flights. **Bay Island Airways** (tel. 504/9858-8819, U.S. tel. 303/242-8004, www.bayislandairways.com) can pick passengers up from La Ceiba, Utila, or Guanaja. Prices are US$250–360 for two people. Island tours are available as well. **Roatan Air Services** (tel. 504/445-1417, Gill García, www.roatanair.com) is another charter service that is said to be a bit flaky at times, but will usually show up if you call to remind them. Prices depend on the size of the plane as well as the route; it's US$185 for Roatán–Utila on a three-passenger (plus pilot) Cessna 172, while the newer Aero Commander costs US$470 but can take up to six passengers.

Apart from rental car stands and a couple of uninspired gift shops, there's not much to hold a traveler's attention at the airport. There is a cigar shop (9 A.M.–5 P.M. Mon.–Fri., 8 A.M.–6 P.M. Sat.–Sun.), which also rents cell phones (US$25/week), although you have to buy the prepaid phone cards elsewhere, due to mysterious airport regulations. There's a small café and an **Espresso Americano** if you need a food or caffeine fix before heading on your way, as well as an ATM and a branch of the travel agency **MC Tours** (tel. 504/445-1930, www.mctours-honduras.com).

The airport is three kilometers from downtown Coxen Hole, on the highway toward French Harbour. Taxis to West End cost US$25, US$5 to Coxen Hole (there is a price sheet posted on one of the columns near the exit). Prices are applicable 6 A.M.–6 P.M.; at other times it's up to your bargaining skills. If you haven't got a whole lot of luggage or cash, it's possible to walk the short distance out to the highway and catch a bus to Coxen Hole, and from there on to West End (US$2). Buses run until about 4 P.M. You can also catch cheaper taxis out here, which charge about US$5 (more or less, depending on your negotiation skills) to West End.

*Note:* When visibility is poor on the north coast due to bad weather (not uncommon for much of the year), the airport at La Ceiba closes with regularity. Don't be surprised to find yourself stranded if the weather turns bad.

## Boat

The **MV Galaxy Wave** (www.safewaymaritime.com) runs daily between La Ceiba and the new Transporte Marítimo Charles McNab dock just east of the Roatán airport; the 90-minute ride costs US$28 (or US$33 for first class). Some snacks are available on the boat, and a movie is shown in the cabin. There is a small coffee shop and gift shop at the ferry dock. The *Galaxy Wave* normally leaves Roatán at 7 A.M. for La Ceiba, then departs from La Ceiba at 9:30 A.M.; it then leaves Roatán again at 2 P.M. and departs from La Ceiba at 4:30 P.M. For more information, call the office in Roatán (tel. 504/445-1795), or in La Ceiba at the Cabotaje dock (tel. 504/443-4633). As with air transport, though not as frequently, the boat is sometimes cancelled due to bad weather. Because the boat is quite large, the ride is pretty smooth, but if the wind has been blowing and the boat goes anyhow, be prepared for some stomach-turning swells. You can get a free antiseasickness pill (à la Dramamine) at the security checkpoint.

If coming from (or heading to) Utila, it might be possible to sail by **catamaran** with Captain Verne Fine (tel. 504/3346-2600). He charges US$50 for the ride and travels back and forth a couple of times per week.

## GETTING AROUND

Roatán has the Bay Islands' only major highway; it runs east–west connecting various island settlements. While the majority of visitors are likely to stay put in West End, West Bay, or the confines of their resort, the more adventurous, and in particular those who don't scuba dive, may wish to explore Roatán's less frequented corners, and this highway offers easy access.

### Bus and Taxi

Most of the island can be covered on Tica minibuses, which leave Coxen Hole frequently from 7 A.M. until 6 P.M. The buses run to Sandy Bay (US$0.75), West End (US$1), French Harbour (US$1), Punta Gorda (US$1.50), and Oak Ridge (US$1.50). All buses leave from the main street in Coxen Hole near the post office, but they will stop anywhere they are hailed (both in town and on the main Roatán road). Be sure to verify the rate *before* stepping onto the bus. Fares must be paid in lempiras.

*Colectivos* (collective taxis) run the same routes for a bit more money—just make sure you clarify that you want a *colectivo*, not a

Roatán's comfortable ferry to La Ceiba, the *Galaxy Wave*

© AMY E. ROBERTSON

private taxi, which will cost considerably more. *Colectivos* stop along the way and pick up whoever flags them down. It's about US$1.50 from the airport to Coxen Hole by *colectivo,* and another US$2 from Coxen Hole to West End. It is virtually impossible to get *colectivo* rates in Coxen Hole on the days the cruise ships are in. After 6 P.M. all rates go up and are negotiable. *Note:* Most taxi drivers are mainlanders who do not speak much English.

Hotels can call for private taxi service when needed, but if you prefer to call directly, a couple of services are: **English Speaking Taxi Drivers** (tel. 504/455-7478), based in French Harbour, and **Roatan Island Cab Service** (tel. 504/445-1882), based in Coxen Hole. The 10-minute ride from West Bay to West End typically costs about US$10.

When negotiating taxi rates, be sure to specify the currency (lempiras or dollars), as the occasional unscrupulous driver may try to take advantage of the obvious tourist.

## Car, Motorcycle, and Bicycle Rental

Several companies rent compact cars and small four-wheel-drive vehicles at rates ranging US$45–75 per day. Many have stands in the airport (sometimes staffed only if they are expecting someone with a reservation), as well as central offices elsewhere on the island, and many will bring the car to your hotel or resort. **Budget** (tel. 504/668-4421, www.budget.com) and **Avis** (tel. 504/445-1568), both at the airport, have a couple of automatic cars—be sure to book in advance if this is what you need—as well as plenty of stick shifts. The best rates can be had by booking through the U.S. website, but be sure to bring a printout of your reservation with you. **Ramirez Rent-A-Car** (tel. 504/445-2228 or 504/9903-9616) has a representative in Coxen Hole at the ferry dock. Two other companies are **Sandy Bay Rent-A-Car** (tel. 504/445-1710 or 504/445-1871, fax 504/445-1711), with offices in Sandy Bay and the airport; and **Caribbean Rent A Car** (tel. 504/445-6950), with an office at the airport (cars start at US$50/day or US$147/week

plus tax). **Roatan Rentals** (tel. 504/445-4171, www.roatansalesandrentals.com), in West End, has a variety of Nissans, Toyotas, Suzukis, Jeep Wranglers, and Trackers for US$50–85 a day. Airport pickups are available only with a rental of a week or more, but West End, West Bay, and Sandy Bay pickups can be easily arranged. Not all cars have air-conditioning.

*Note:* Sign a contract only for the number of days you are absolutely sure you want, as it can be very difficult to get any money back if you end up turning the car in early. You may also want to take a look at the car before signing the contract if you are with a lesser-known company. While most are reputable, there have been some reports of cars being in less than tip-top condition, and it's good to know what you're getting into.

**Captain Van's** (www.captainvans.com, 9 A.M.–4 P.M. daily), in West End (tel. 504/445-4076) and at the West Bay Mall (tel. 504/445-5040), rents motorcycles for US$45–55 a day, scooters for US$39 a day, and mountain bikes for US$9 a day. Weekly rates are available, and they provide maps, helmets, and information on the best spots on the island. Cell phones, DVD players, and DVDs are available for rent as well at the West Bay location.

## Tour Operators

**TransTours** (tel. 504/9928-6579, www.transtoursroatan.com) offers tours around the islands for US$25 per person (for a group of four; discount of $5 pp for larger groups), as well as day trips to the mainland to hike in Pico Bonito or river raft on the Río Cangrejal, and overnight trips to the ruins of Copán.

## ACCOMMODATIONS

There is something to suit absolutely every budget and taste on Roatán, from US$10 dorms to the extravagant US$22,500 six-bedroom Mayoka Lodge. Many house vacation rentals are available across the island. A few are listed here, or try Roatan Life Vacation Rentals (tel. 504/445-3130, U.S. tel. 970/300-4078, www.roatanlifevacationrentals.com) for a larger selection, of both short-term rentals and

## ◖ DIVING ROATÁN'S REEF

an underwater jungle of coral

The reef topography in Roatán, as with Utila and Guanaja, is divided into a north side and a south side. On the north side of the island, the reef is separated from shore by a shallow lagoon, sometimes a kilometer wide but usually less. From the crest, which sometimes almost breaks the water's surface, the reef slopes down to a plateau or moat, followed by the reef wall. On the north side, sponges, sea fans, and elkhorn coral are common. The south-side reef slopes out gently until reaching the edge of the wall, normally dropping from 10 meters down to 30 meters, with a sandy bottom. Here grow a bewildering assortment of colorful soft corals. On the western end of the island, where the north- and south-side reefs meet, the reef shows characteristics of both formations.

The most popular dive sites in Roatán are in the Sandy Bay Marine Reserve, a protected water reserve between Sandy Bay and West Bay on the western end of the island, conveniently near the dive shops in West End. The reefs on the northern, eastern, and southern sides of Roatán have many spectacular, infrequently visited sites — the best bet is stay at one of the resorts out that way, or ask around in West End for shops diving more remote sites. While dive shops often have a site in mind, some are open to requests by divers.

### NEAR WEST END

**Hole in the Wall,** a crack in the reef just around the bend from Half Moon Bay on the way to Sandy Bay, is justifiably one of the favorite dives near West End. Cruise down a steep sand chute from the upper reef, which leads downward through a cleft and pops out on the reef wall at around 40 meters. Below is very dark water — here is one of the places the Cayman Trench comes in closest to Roatán, and water depths just below Hole in the Wall are around 800 meters. Keep a close eye on that depth gauge. While the wall is the obvious highlight of the dive, leave time to explore around the labyrinth of sand chutes on the

long-term leases. There are also listings on the website for Subway Watersports (www.subway watersports.com).

## BOATING

The clear, clean waters surrounding Roatán, stroked by steady trade winds most of the year and stocked with most of the known fish species in the Caribbean, are superb for sailing and fishing trips. The Bay Islands are a growing destination among the yacht crowd, although docking services are limited to Barefoot Cay on Roatán, and in La Ceiba.

Many boat owners offer fishing trips, either deep-sea or flats fishing, or both. Day trips, cocktail cruises, and other customized boat trips can be arranged. One of the easiest ways to get what you are looking for is simply upper reef, where you might spot a barracuda or eagle ray.

Right out front of West End is **Blue Channel,** a canyon with a narrow opening that gradually widens and deepens as you swim away from shore. A mellow dive, good for the afternoon, the channel has swim-throughs, interesting rock and coral formations, and plenty of fish to watch. Look for a green moray that hangs out near the entrance to the channel.

Off the southwest point of Roatán is **West End Wall.** Because of its location, strong currents flow past the site, meaning divers need to plan a drift dive. While the wall is worth seeing, it's also fun just to let the current zip you across the reef fields above the wall, which are invariably filled with hawksbill turtles, spotted eagle rays, and a dazzling array of colorful fish.

### NEAR SANDY BAY
Near Anthony's Key Resort is the wreck of *El Aguila,* a 71-meter freighter the resort bought and sank in sand flats at 34 meters, near the base of the reef wall, to create a dive site. Take good care not to catch yourself on any metal parts as you swim around the deck – and look for the green moray and large grouper that live at the site.

Just east of Anthony's Key, right in front of Sandy Bay, is **Bear's Den,** a cave system lit from above. The cave entrance, on the upper part of a steep reef wall decorated with much boulder and lettuce coral, is tight to get in but widens out into a spacious cavern inside. Beautiful, shifting light from above illuminates schools of glassy-eyed sweepers that patrol the cave. The cave system continues farther,

but only experienced cave divers should continue beyond the main cavern.

**Spooky Channel,** at the eastern end of Sandy Bay, is exactly what it sounds like, a channel through the reef almost completely closed over, and a bit unnerving to swim through for the dark water. The dive starts at 12 meters or so and deepens as you go in to a maximum of about 38 meters. While rock and fossilized coral predominate in the lower reaches of the channel, up higher on the reef barrel sponges, sea fans, and hard corals are common.

### ELSEWHERE ON THE ISLAND
Considered one of the most dramatic dives on Roatán, **Mary's Place,** just west of French Harbour on the south side, is a narrow cleft in the reef wall. Enter at around 25 meters, then zigzag into the cleft, where you'll see plenty of large sponges and also lots of seahorses. Because of the tight channels, Mary's Place is for experienced divers only.

Right in front of Coco View Resort, east of French Harbour, is **Valley of the Kings,** an exceptionally lovely wall dive noted for the tall stands of pillar coral, several different types of sponge, and a profusion of marine life tucked into crevasses and overhangs on the wall.

### OTHER RECOMMENDED DIVES
Other sites around the island that are highly recommended by divers who know the Roatán reef well include: Mandy's Eel Garden, Lighthouse Reef, Half Moon Bay Wall, Fish Den, Canyon Reef, Odyssey Wreck, Peter's Place, Pablo's Place, and Front Porch.

to ask around, or keep an eye out for posted fliers offering cruises. **Roatan Sailboat and Catamaran Charters** (tel. 504/3336-5597 or U.S. tel. 813/435-6337, www.sailroatan.com) has various options available, from a three-hour sail for US$65 per person to seven-day sail and dive packages. **Captain Dusty** also runs daily five-hour snorkel and sail trips for US$49 per person, beer and gear included.

### ◖ Fishing
Situated at the division between the shallow waters toward the mainland on one side and the 3,000-meter-deep Cayman Channel on the other, Roatán and the other Bay Islands are ideally located to go after a variety of different shallow- and deep-water species. Favorite game fish around Roatán are marlin, wahoo, tarpon, barracuda, kingfish, and jack, to name just a

few. Waters around most major settlements are usually heavily fished by the locals, so more isolated spots, particularly on the north and east sides of the island, offer the best luck.

Captain Loren Monterrosa of **Early Bird Fishing Charter** (tel. 504/445-3019, or 504/9955-0001, www.earlybirdfishingcharters.com), in Sandy Bay, offers deep-sea and flats fishing as well as island tours and trips to Utila. Half-day deep-sea fishing trips cost US$350–400 (up to four people, including drinks, snacks, and fruit), and full-day trips cost US$600 (up to four people, including drinks, snacks, fruit, and lunch). Fishing trips can also be arranged with **Hook 'Em Up** (tel. 504/9919-7603, www.westendroatan.com/hookup.htm), run by top-notch local fisherman Captain "O" Miller, who can also be found by asking at Diddily's gift shop near the church in West End. He charges US$65–75 per hour for fishing trips, and also does snorkeling outings (US$20 pp per hour) and island tours (from US$300). **Eddie and Donna's Fishing Charters** (tel. 504/9653-1293 or 504/9553-3302), in West End, charges US$150 (up to six people) for six-hour trips on their small boat (a *lancha*) and US$350 (up to 10 people) on their larger boat, including snorkeling and drinks. On the smaller boat, a tour through the mangroves can be included as well. Other fishermen in West End, West Bay, Sandy Bay, or elsewhere will also happily set up fishing trips for a negotiable fee.

## Marina and Boat Services

Yachties can tie up in Roatán at **Barefoot Cay** (tel. 504/455-6235, VHF Channel 18A, www.barefootcay.com), between French Harbour and Brick Bay, charging US$1.25 per foot per day, or US$18 per foot per month. Boats up to 165 feet can be accommodated; water and electricity are extra.

## WEST END

Although it is the main tourist town of Roatán and lined with cabañas, restaurants, and dive shops, West End remains a slow-paced seaside village and an undeniably superb location to lose yourself in the relaxing rhythms

of Caribbean life. Even during the high season (mid-December–April), people and events move at a languid pace up and down the sandy, seaside road that constitutes "town." It's a telling sign that the road has been left rutted and unpaved—cars and bicycles must slow to a snail's pace, bouncing along, while pedestrians are free to wander at leisure, stopping to browse for T-shirts or to admire yet another spectacular sunset.

Construction of new houses and cabañas continues, but in a relatively unobtrusive way—new developments are tucked away among the palms and don't dominate the visual landscape. West End is not overwhelmed by wealthy tourists, as it has no luxury resorts, but there are a few higher-end options for those who prefer a few more comforts. The roughly 500 local residents have not lost their easy friendliness and, fortunately, seem to be influencing the newcomers more than the newcomers are influencing them.

### Sights

West End's main attractions are in plain view: beaches, 28°C (82°F) bright-blue water, and, a couple hundred meters offshore, the coral reef, marked by a chain of buoys. The waters around West End are kept very clean, and visitors can jump in pretty much wherever it's convenient. The best beach in town is **Half Moon Bay,** a swath of palm-lined sand right at the entrance to West End, bordered by points of iron shore (fossilized, raised coral) on either side forming the namesake shape. A good spot to lay down a towel is in the stretch in front of the Posada Arco Iris hotel. Another good place to swim and sunbathe is off the docks at the far south end of town, just after the road ends. Both of these spots happen to be near two good snorkeling sites off West End. The reef passes right across the mouth of Half Moon Bay, an easy swim from shore, with better reef near the more southern of the two points. Sea turtles and rays are often seen in the sand flats and shallower sections of reef here.

One of the buoys in front of the south end of the town beach marks the entrance to **Blue**

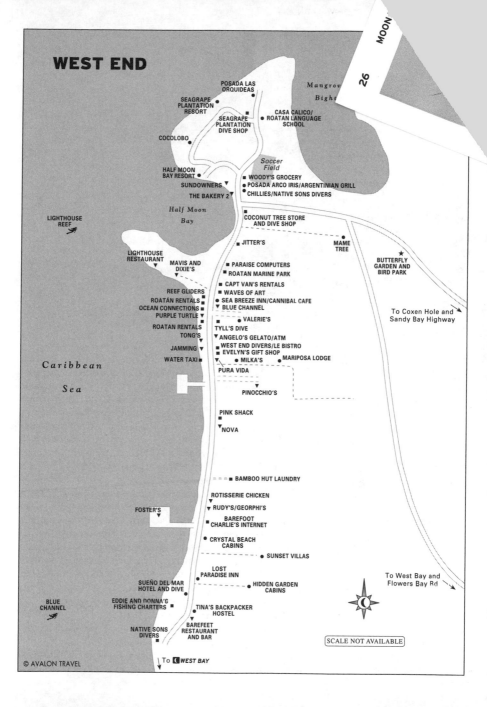

# WEST END

POSADA LAS ORQUIDEAS

*Mangrov* *Bight*

26 MOON

SEAGRAPE PLANTATION RESORT

CASA CALICO/ ROATAN LANGUAGE SCHOOL

SEAGRAPE PLANTATION DIVE SHOP

COCOLOBO

*Soccer Field*

HALF MOON BAY RESORT

WOODY'S GROCERY

SUNDOWNERS

POSADA ARCO IRIS/ARGENTINIAN GRILL

THE BAKERY 2

CHILLIES/NATIVE SONS DIVERS

*Half Moon Bay*

COCONUT TREE STORE AND DIVE SHOP

LIGHTHOUSE REEF

JITTER'S

MAME TREE

★ BUTTERFLY GARDEN AND BIRD PARK

LIGHTHOUSE RESTAURANT

MAVIS AND DIXIE'S

PARAISE COMPUTERS

ROATAN MARINE PARK

REEF GLIDERS

CAPT VAN'S RENTALS

ROATÁN RENTALS

WAVES OF ART

OCEAN CONNECTIONS

SEA BREEZE INN/CANNIBAL CAFE

To Coxen Hole and Sandy Bay Highway

PURPLE TURTLE

BLUE CHANNEL

ROATAN RENTALS

VALERIE'S

TONG'S

TYLL'S DIVE

ANGELO'S GELATO/ATM

JAMMING

WEST END DIVERS/LE BISTRO

EVELYN'S GIFT SHOP

WATER TAXI

MILKA'S

MARIPOSA LODGE

*Caribbean*

PURA VIDA

*Sea*

PINOCCHIO'S

PINK SHACK

NOVA

BAMBOO HUT LAUNDRY

ROTISSERIE CHICKEN

FOSTER'S

RUDY'S/GEORPHI'S

BAREFOOT CHARLIE'S INTERNET

CRYSTAL BEACH CABINS

SUNSET VILLAS

LOST PARADISE INN

To West Bay and Flowers Bay Rd

SUEÑO DEL MAR HOTEL AND DIVE

HIDDEN GARDEN CABINS

BLUE CHANNEL

EDDIE AND DONNA'S FISHING CHARTERS

TINA'S BACKPACKER HOSTEL

NATIVE SONS DIVERS

BAREFEET RESTAURANT AND BAR

SCALE NOT AVAILABLE

To **C** WEST BAY

© AVALON TRAVEL

Docks sprinkled along the shoreline are perfect spots for taking in the view.

© AMY E. ROBERTSON

**Channel,** a dramatic channel cutting through the reef. It's a bit of a swim for snorkelers, so take your time heading out to conserve energy for exploring the reef and the trip back.

There are several other sites on the reef off West End, but in looking for them beware of boat traffic. Snorkel gear can be rented from many of the dive shops for US$7, or a bit less from stores in town, like the gift shop at the **Roatan Marine Park** office. A passport or US$10–15 deposit is usually required.

## Dive Shops

West End's fully equipped dive shops offer dives and courses for all levels and in several languages. Courses and dive packages should cost close to the same everywhere: US$280–325 for the standard or Advanced Open Water certifications, US$100 for a half-day Discover Scuba Diving course, US$35 for a fun dive, and US$25–30 per dive for 10 or more dives. Prices can fluctuate somewhat with the season and have risen slightly over the years. Generally, all shops have three dives daily—one at 9 A.M.,

one at 11 A.M., and one at 2 P.M. (although some run dives half an hour earlier or later)—and start new certification courses every couple of days. Apart from the shops listed, there are a few outfits based out of West Bay, for people who prefer to stay there. Fun dive prices typically do not include equipment, which can tack on another US$5–15.

**Coconut Tree Divers** (tel. 504/403-8782, www.coconuttreedivers.com), in the same building as the Coconut Tree Store in front of Half Moon Bay, has plenty of good gear, a well-equipped 40-foot dive boat, and an air-conditioned classroom. The PADI-certified shop can pick up guests in their West Bay accommodations for morning and afternoon dives. They offer Nitrox and instructor courses as well. Equipment rental is included in their fun dives (US$35 each).

**Native Sons Divers** (tel. 504/445-4003, www.nativesonsroatan.com) has offices on the beach at the south end of town and at Chillies Hotel. Native Sons is a frequently recommended, locally run shop certified with PADI and providing experienced instructors. The shop can also arrange fishing trips.

**Ocean Connections** (tel. 504/403-8221, www.ocean-connections.com), a well-respected dive shop, has equipment for Nitrox and other technical dive training, as well as the standard courses and dive tours. PADI classifies it as a Gold Palm dive center, in recognition of the shop's quality and volume of business.

**Pura Vida** (tel. 504/445-4130, U.S. tel. 786/319-4571, www.puravidaresort.com), another PADI five-star Gold Palm resort-rated shop, has three boats, an air-conditioned classroom, and a spacious wooden porch for hanging out.

**Reef Gliders** (tel. 504/403-8243, www.reefgliders.com) is run by an English couple who rebuilt the two dive boats, bought new gear, and refurbished the shop. The reputable Reef Gliders offers all of the courses through Dive Master, as well as numerous specialties. Penny-pinchers will be happy to find that free dorm-style accommodation is offered to dive students—but at the rather run-down Valerie's hotel in town.

**Seagrape Plantation** (tel. 504/445-4297, www.seagraperoatan.com) is well-located for visitors staying at any of the hotels on the point, such as Posada las Orquideas, Cocolobo, and Casa Calico.

**Sueño del Mar** (tel. 504/445-4343, www.suenodelmar.com), housed in a large building out on its own private dock in the West End harbor, has a dive shop on the "ground" floor and a popular restaurant/bar above. The shop has two skiffs and a boat kept at Brick Bay to dive on the south side. Sueño has about the best dive gear shop on the island. They offer lodging and dive packages, with rooms both at what they call the Roatan West End Hotel (a.k.a. the Sea Breeze Inn), in the middle of town for a bargain basement US$411 per week, and in their relatively new, white-washed resort lodge on the south end of town right on the water, with breezy tile-floored rooms, a very good value at US$550 per person per week.

**Tyll's Dive** (tel. 504/403-8852, www.tyllsdive.com) is one of the oldest shops in West End. It offers a full range of courses in a variety of languages, and prices are on the lower end of the scale.

**West End Divers** (tel. 504/445-4289, www.westenddivers.com) is known for diving a larger variety of sites and venturing farther out than some of the other shops. The fun dives at West End cost a bit more (US$40 each, or US$30 when purchased in a package of 10 or more), but the course prices are competitive.

## Snorkeling

Snorkel equipment is available for rent at the offices of the Roatan Marine Park (US$5 for 24 hours), as well as at the Sea Breeze Inn (US$5 for 4 hours) and at many of the dive shops.

## Other Recreation

While diving and snorkeling are justifiably premier attractions on Roatán, there are plenty of other excellent water and land-based activities, many based in West End.

**Sea kayaks** are available for rent at the Sea Breeze Inn (tel. 504/445-4026), for US$7 an hour for a double. Half-day rentals cost US$18, and full-day rentals cost US$21. *Note:* Visitors should take good care when paddling out into the open water on sea kayaks. Choppy waters and ocean winds can quickly get the better of inexperienced kayakers. If in any doubt at all, stick close to shore and be absolutely sure you have enough energy not only to get out, but to get back, too.

**Glass-bottomed boat tours** (US$30 for an hour) leave from a dock on the southern half of town—look for the sign, and double-check on the schedule, as it varies with the seasons. Trips are also available from West Bay Beach, a quick water taxi ride away.

Half Moon Bay has a pretty beach, perfect for a relaxing afternoon. Those looking for a spectacular Caribbean beach should catch a **water taxi** over to West Bay for its seemingly endless stretch of powdery white sand (US$2.50 for the 10-minute ride).

Fishing trips can be arranged with a number of local fishermen; one to try is **Eddie and Donna's Fishing Charters** (tel. 504/9653-1293) on the beach just after the road ends at the southern end of town. Six-hour trips on a boat that can take 6–10 guests run US$350, while a trip on a fiberglass *lancha* is US$150 and can include a tour through the mangroves. Be sure to bring lots of sunscreen for either excursion, as well as your snorkel gear. They also provide water taxi service to West Bay.

Just east of West End on the road to Coxen Hole, walkable if you watch out for traffic, is the **Butterfly Garden and Bird Park** (tel. 504/445-4481, www.roatanbutterfly.com, 9 A.M.–5 P.M. Sun.–Fri., US$7), with a collection of 18 or so butterfly species as well as a few toucans, parrots, and macaws. It's a modest little collection, but a break from all the water-oriented recreations if you're in the mood for something different.

There are a couple of canopy tours available just outside of town, on the road to West Bay.

## Entertainment

Perhaps the most popular spot in town for a sunset drink, **C Sundowners Bar and Restaurant** (10 A.M.–10 P.M. daily), on the beach across the road from Chillies Hotel, draws a mellow crowd of tourists looking for good vibes and a good variety of drinks.

Another favored spot for a drink, the **Purple Turtle** (tel. 504/445-4483, 7 P.M.–midnight Mon.–Thurs., 7 P.M.–2 A.M. Fri.–Sat., 7–10 P.M. Sun.) is a tiny bar featuring a small porch area in back with hammock chairs overlooking the sea, popular with long-haired, laid-back types.

**Nova's** is a new lounge-style bar (read: low-slung couches) with '80s night on Wednesdays, techno/electronic music on Fridays, and Latin music on Saturdays. Happy hour is 7–8 P.M., when well drinks are just a buck. Another newcomer to West End's nightlife scene is **Jamming,** a small bar built out over the water's edge, with reggae music and a relaxed vibe day and night (the relaxation aided, no doubt, by drink specials such as US$1.80 tequila shots).

**Foster's** (tel. 504/377-6304, noon–midnight Mon.–Thurs., noon–2 A.M. Fri.–Sat., and noon–10 P.M. Sun.) is an unpretentious hangout that draws a jovial crowd of locals and expats as well as tourists on Friday and Saturday nights. The restaurant/bar is a two-story wooden contraption built on a dock over the water, with a couple of hammocks swinging between the wood beams. It's a shame the place is empty the rest of the week. Happy hour is 4–6 P.M.

The restaurant **Blue Channel** (tel. 504/445-4133) has live music Wednesday–Saturday and frequently shows movies; details are posted on the board out front. **Le Bistro** also has live music on Fridays and Saturdays.

The second-floor bar at **Sueño del Mar** dive shop, a large white building at the southern end of town, is a fine place to nurse a drink and watch the sun take its invariably sublime daily plunge into the Caribbean. There's also a large-screen TV to watch sports.

If you have the energy to keep going when everything closes down, try to track down a cab to take you to **Hip Hop** in Flowers Bay, near Coxen Hole—just don't arrive before 2 A.M. or you'll be the only one there.

## Shopping

**Pink Shack,** in the southern half of town, sells T-shirts with their own quite clever designs, as well as a few other items such as flip-flops and Crocs.

**Waves of Art** (tel. 504/403-8819, 9 A.M.–6 P.M. Mon., Tues., and Sat., 9 A.M.–8 P.M. Wed.–Fri., www.waves-of-art.com), located in a Victorian-style building across from the church, offers art and handicrafts that promote sustainable living among low-income Hondurans, including candles, carvings, note cards, and jewelry made by co-ops from across the country. The upstairs gallery features art in numerous media, including paintings, photos, sculptures, and metal works, and hosts new gallery showings every six weeks. Credit cards are accepted.

A number of Guatemalan artisans have made their way to the Bay Islands to sell their fine handicrafts; **Evelyn Gift Shop,** next door to the Pura Vida Dive Shop, has a good selection of both Guatemalan and Honduran crafts.

## Accommodations

Hotels in West End mostly fall into the moderate range, US$25–50 for a double, generally in a cabin with ceiling fan, screened windows, and private bathroom. The budget traveler will be glad to hear, however, that less expensive digs are still available—although groups of two or three can often find better quality rooms for the same price in the midrange accommodations. There are a couple of higher end spots, too, for those who prefer the buzz of West End over the quiet nights on West Bay beach or at the resorts. Keep in mind that the lower-end prices are available September–November. The 16 percent Honduran tax on hotel rooms has been added here for those hotels that do not include it in their rates. It's worth keeping in mind that hotels that normally charge separately for the tax are often willing to include it in their rates for guests who pay with cash.

For those who become transfixed with diving and the mellow lifestyle in West End, locals rent many apartments and cabins of differing quality for about US$350–800 a month, more in the high season. Rents in nearby locations like Gibson Bight and Sandy Bay are lower.

### UNDER US$25

The best low-budget room in town is at **Ⓒ Georphi's** (tel. 504/445-4205, www.roatan georphis.com), where one cabin has been converted into a tidy, attractive dorm (US$10 pp) with (gasp!) hot water in the shared bath.

A good alternative for backpackers is **Tina's Backpacker Hostel** (tel. 504/445-4144, moy-1978@yahoo.com, cold water only) at the southern end of town just where the road becomes beach. Dorm beds go for US$10 per person, and the place is clean and cheery. There are two rooms with four beds each, plus another two pairs of beds in the shared living room with a TV, so better nab your bed as soon as possible if you're early to bed. There is a kitchen available for use by guests. The hostel is run by the owners of the adjacent Barefeet Restaurant and Bar.

**Chillies Hotel** (tel. 504/445-4003, US$20–24 s/d, US$27–30 t, shared bath, cold water),

facing Half Moon Bay, is very popular with the low-budget crowd, for its doubles with shared bathroom and kitchen facilities as well as a sociable front porch. There are also a few rooms with private baths and hot water for a few dollars more, available only to those diving with their dive shop, Native Sons.

**Milka's** (tel. 504/445-4241, milkasrooms@ yahoo.com, US$12 pp shared bath, US$25 d with bath and TV, cold water only), located behind Pura Vida, is a bit ramshackle but offers 11 very basic rooms with fans and shared bathrooms, as well as three much better rooms with TV and private bathrooms.

One of the cheapest places in town is **Valerie's** (tel. 504/3290-6055), a run-down hotel in the center of town with dorms for US$8, doubles with bath for US$16, and apartments with refrigerator, cooktop, and bath for US$25. It's all cold-water only and rather grubby.

Many local residents rent rooms out of their houses for US$10–25 d—ask around.

### US$25-50

Half a block north from the entrance to town is the highly recommended **Ⓒ Posada Arco Iris** (tel./fax 504/445-4264, www.roatanposada.com, US$36–48 s, US$42–54 d), run by an Argentinian couple. The spacious and clean rooms in the wooden house are each decorated with colorful artistic touches. The top-floor ocean-view rooms facing Half Moon Bay are the more expensive rooms, and some have kitchens. The individual wooden cabins, with ample front porches, rent for US$66 (one bedroom) and US$78 (two bedroom) for two people during high season. All accommodations cost US$15 more per day with air-conditioning. Out front is a very good Argentine-style restaurant.

**The Sea Breeze Inn** (tel. 504/445-4026, www.seabreezeroatan.com, US$25–70 d), at the entrance to town, has a variety of room layouts including studios and suites that can accommodate larger parties with a little bit of privacy. The standard rooms are fairly charmless, and the grounds are rather cramped, but there are a few rooms with porches, hammocks, and kitchenettes. Kayaks and snorkel equipment are available for rent.

In a rambling three-story wooden house built atop a small hill a couple of hundred meters back off the main road, behind Pura Vida, is **Mariposa Lodge** (tel. 504/445-4450, www.mariposa-lodge.com, US$40 s/d, US$55 t, two-night minimum for all rooms), with four simple but spacious apartments with a homey feel, all with private kitchens, TV, fans, and hot water, as well as a breezy porch to relax on. In addition, there's a small house with three rooms that rent for US$26 d, with fan, hot water, and shared bathroom and kitchen facilities—a bit worn, but decent. The Canadian couple who own the place also offer professional shiatsu, therapeutic, and reiki massage service (very popular with the diving crowd) for US$40 an hour.

Located on the second floor, above the restaurant of the same name, the rooms at **Pinocchio's** (tel. 504/445-4466, or 504/9837-7287, US$35 s/d, US$10 each additional person) are a good value. Each has wood floors and walls, two double beds, and hot water. Breakfast at the restaurant downstairs is included, and the dinners there are top-notch. Don't worry about noise from the restaurant, as it closes by 10 P.M. at the latest.

**◖ Georphi's** (tel. 504/445-4205, www.roatangeorphis.com), located next to Rudy's restaurant, is named for owners George and Phyllis. The rambling grounds, dotted with tropical plants, feature a number of individual wooden cabins with spacious porches. Prices start at US$25 for one room in a two-bedroom cabin with fan, and go up to US$50 for cabins with more space and air-conditioning; most have kitchenettes. There is even a small chalet available, with a king bed in a bedroom and a twin bed in the loft, and extra beds can be added for more kids (US$75/night, or US$850/month). One cabin has been converted into a dorm, the best low-budget digs in town, for US$10 per person. Internet is available in the lobby (US$3/day or US$10/week), there is free wireless Internet

on the grounds, and laundry service is available too.

Another good choice for cabins is **Hidden Garden Cabins** (tel. 504/445-4131, www.hiddengardencabins.com, US$45 s/d, US$250/week), also set back from the road in lush vegetation, each with hot water, a kitchen, and a porch. Ceiling fans help keep the island breezes moving through the slat windows.

At the edge of town along Mangrove Bight is **Posada Las Orquideas** (tel. 504/445-4387, www.posadalasorquideas.com, US$36–60 d, plus an extra US$15 for a/c), with absolutely lovely rooms in a large wooden building set along the iron shore, an excellent deal if you are looking to get away at the end of the day (although it's only about a 10-minute walk, it's can feel like a bit of a hike, particularly late at night). The PADI-certified Seagrape Dive Shop (tel. 504/445-4297) is just steps away (and charges a few bucks less for its fun dives than its competitors in town).

## US$50-100

**Half Moon Resort** (tel. 504/445-4242, www.roatanhalfmoonresort.com, US$67 s/d), on the quiet northern point of Half Moon Bay, offers somewhat spartan wooden waterfront cabins with air-conditioning and hot water. The cabins closest to the water are the best—enjoy views of Half Moon Bay from your porch hammock. Guests can use free kayaks and snorkel gear in the small bay and reef right out front, the seafood at the porch restaurant is reliable, and the staff is an amiable bunch. The hotel's access to the beach is via iron shore (calcified coral reef).

On the same land outcropping as Half Moon Resort, but facing Mangrove Bight rather than Half Moon Bay, is the surprisingly woodsy **Hotel Casa Calico** (tel. 504/445-4231, US$70–90 for rooms that sleep up to five). The spacious rooms have kitchenettes, tables, and TVs, while smaller rooms that start at US$50 still boast balconies and deck chairs. Two-bedroom condos with full kitchens are also available for US$125–150. The lack of beach at this waterfront property may be a disappointment for some, but kayaks are available for getting into the water right at the shoreline, among the mangroves. Pleasant and roomy one-bedroom apartments with daily and monthly rates are available, especially convenient for those taking Spanish classes through the hotel's **Roatan Language School**. It's a 10-minute walk to the restaurants in the heart of town.

Right in the center of town is **Pura Vida** (tel. 504/445-4110, U.S. tel. 786/319-4571, www.puravidaresort.com, US$74 s, US$90 d), with clean, airy, tile-floored rooms with hot water, air-conditioning, and TV. The hotel has 26 rooms and a rather ordinary restaurant. Three-day and seven-day packages, including diving and breakfast, are also available.

A long-time resident of West End, **Lost Paradise Inn** (tel. 504/445-4210 or 504/445-4306, www.lost-paradise.com, US$79 s/d) rents rooms in well-made wooden cabins on stilts in a nice layout right on the beach in the south end of town. Rooms are equipped with air-conditioning, small refrigerators, and hot water, and some have small porches. Many have two double beds and can sleep up to four. A restaurant operates in the high season only.

**US$100 AND UP**

**Mame Tree Bungalows** (tel. 504/403-8245, U.S. tel. 718/710-4392, www.mametree bungalows.com) is set on a bluff above town, just a minute or two's walk along a hillside path from West End's main drag and beach, a perfect place for being close to the hubbub of town without being in the middle of it. The two main bungalows have two bedrooms and can sleep up to five each (US$157 with a view, or US$133 without), while new smaller rooms are perfect for romantic couples (US$68–80). The young American owners have decorated with a lot of character (mosaic tiling in the Caribbean room, lush fabrics in the Moroccan), as well as with luxury touches such as flat-screen TVs, wireless Internet, and soundproofed walls.

Although only a short path separates

Half Moon Resort from [...] 504/9898-4510, www.coco[...] d, including breakfast), this ne[...] removed from the hustle and bu[...] End. Rooms have a sweeping view o[...] shore and ocean. Conceived by a Briti[...] vironmental architect, the wood structu[...] are designed with windows that create cooling cross-breezes—but the air-conditioning is there for those who can't live without it. Luxury touches include an infinity-edged pool, flat-screen TVs, and iPod docks, but the vibe is relaxed, perfect for grown-up beach bums. Small apartments are also available on a weekly basis, with peek-a-boo ocean views.

A big whitewashed development set back a few steps from the main road is the well-appointed **Sunset Villas** (tel. 504/445-4100, U.S. tel. 603/782-4470, www.roatanhotels .com, US$75–98 s/d). Hotel rooms are in a building above the large pool, and are outfitted with either a king bed or two doubles, as well as attractively tiled bathrooms, flat-screen TVs, and a mini-fridge (suites with kitchens cost US$30 more). Spacious and fairly deluxe one- and two-bedroom condos with Tommy Bahama furniture and full kitchens are available for US$153–276 (if you know what Tommy Bahama is, then this is the place for you).

## Food
### BREAKFAST
One choice breakfast spot in town is **Rudy's** (6 A.M.–5 P.M. Sun.–Fri.), next to Georphi's hotel, where the owner, if he's there, will serve you up a steaming cup of coffee and invariably reply heartily, "Still alive!" when you ask how he's doing. The response is so famous it appears on a specially made T-shirt. The omelets are excellent (you pick the fixings), US$2–4. The smoothies (US$4) are outrageously priced if you're used to mainland *licuados,* but good nonetheless.

Conveniently located in the center of town, **Jitters** (8 A.M.–2:30 P.M. Mon.–Fri., 8 A.M.–noon Sun.) serves up a nice latte, as well as refreshing iced coffees and smoothies, and a few

**C Cocolobo** (tel.
...obo.com, US$122
...w hotel feels far
...tle of West
...the iron
...en-
...es

...utter brownies
...m. Mon.–Fri.,
... for its filling
...ast with house-
...lads, and burg-
...$5–8). The best
...mall waterfront

## SNACKS AND LIGHT MEALS

At the entrance to Georphi's Hotel is **Creole's Rotisserie Chicken,** serving up quarter-chickens for US$3.70, whole chickens for US$9.50, and sides for two bucks apiece.

Along the beach by Posada Arco Iris is an authentic British **fish and chip truck,** where a plate goes for US$7–8.

The *baleadas* sold next to Ocean Connections dive shop are especially good, and always a cheap way to fill up.

Looking to cool off, or to satisfy a sweet tooth? **Angelo's Gelato** has a small selection of good ice cream, US$1.50 for one scoop, US$2.50 for two.

## SEAFOOD

A locally run restaurant specializing in fresh islander food is **C The Lighthouse Restaurant** (7:30 A.M.–10 P.M. daily, no credit cards accepted), located on the south side of the point dividing the main part of West End from Half Moon Bay. A sign on the main road points the way to the classy patio restaurant, right on the water. Fresh fish and shrimp are served in a variety of ways, including with the fiery *escabey* sauce made with lots of hot island peppers, US$8–13. The more extravagant "surf and turf" and seafood platters are US$20–30. The menu is extensive, and it's all good. Lunch is a particularly good deal, with specials such as grouper burgers and lobster avocado salad. A champagne brunch is served on Sundays for US$15.

The waterfront porch at **Half Moon Resort** (tel. 504/445-4242) is a fine location to enjoy mouthwatering fish fillets, lobster, shrimp, and other seafood. Dinners run US$8–14 and are worth every penny. Large chicken or fish sandwiches with fries cost US$6. The kitchen is open daily until 10 P.M.

Pleasantly set along the beach in the center of town, **Mavis and Dixie's** has excellent shrimp, fish, and lobster for reasonable prices, and a US$6 plate of the day.

Located at the southern end of town right on the beach is **Barefeet Restaurant and Bar,** a casual joint with sandwiches (US$5–8) as well as seafood, meat and pasta (US$10–16), and even king crab (US$19). There is a Sunday barbecue with live music, and happy hour every day 3–7 P.M.

## INTERNATIONAL

If all this fish has got you hankering after a steak for a change, stop in at **Argentinian Grill** (tel. 504/445-4264, 3–10 P.M. Thurs.–Tues.), at the Posada Arco Iris, and try the beef tenderloin or the filet mignon for around US$16, or a *chorizo* sausage. Even the half portion of meat, served with a twice-baked potato and veggies for US$13, is a generous plate. Don't worry if your companion isn't a meat-eater, as there's vegetarian lasagna and a daily vegetarian plate. Good seafood is, of course, also available, served with Argentine *chimichurri* sauce for variety.

**C Pinocchio's** (tel. 504/445-4466 or 504/9837-7287, 6–9 P.M. Tues.–Fri.) is tucked a hundred meters or so off the main road in West End, but well worth seeking out for the excellent, unusual dishes, such as beef tenderloin with sesame and merlot reduction, and its intriguing selection of *tapas*. Prices are not cheap (US$11–20 per plate), but it's great for a splurge. The new European owners include a pastry chef from the Netherlands, who makes desserts to die for, such as a plum tart with earl grey mascarpone.

The **Blue Channel** (tel. 504/445-4133) offers movie screenings and frequent live music along with its Italian-style pastas. The breakfasts are good too.

Featuring Tex-Mex dishes such as tacos, quesadillas, fajitas, and chimichangas, for about US$3.50–5, **Cannibal Café** (tel. 504/445-4026, 9 A.M.–10 P.M. Mon.–Sat.) is in front of the Sea Breeze Inn—you can't miss the life-like "cannibal" sitting out front. The "big Kahuna burrito" is famously large; if you can stuff down three within an hour, they'll give them to you for free.

## ASIAN

Opposite Jamming, **Le Bistro** (3–10 P.M. daily, also open for lunch during high season) is a Thai-Vietnamese restaurant with dishes you won't find anywhere else in Honduras, such as *blau blau,* Vietnamese hotpot, as well as plenty of more familiar dishes such as spring rolls and pad thai. The restaurant is on a second-story wood deck, and rather atmospheric, although the thumping music from Jamming tends to drown out the crooning French music in the background. Appetizers are US$2–6, and most mains are in the range of US$8–16.

**Tong's Thai Cuisine** (5:30–9:30 P.M. daily, plus open for lunch Fri.–Sun.) is a relatively new restaurant set out over the water, wildly popular for its excellent Thai food. The curries and basil chicken are authentically spicy, while those looking for something milder will be happy with the fried rice. Entrées run US$12–18. The staffing has yet to catch up with the restaurant's popularity, so if the restaurant is busy you can expect your food to take a good long while (or consider coming when the crowds are gone).

## GROCERIES

The best, and really only, grocery store in West End is **Woody's** (tel. 504/445-4269, 7 A.M.–6 P.M. Sun.–Thurs., 6 A.M.–8:30 P.M. Fri., and 7 A.M.–5 P.M. Sat.), with a decent selection of packaged goods and the occasional, slightly limp-looking vegetable. Eldon's in French Harbour and Coxen Hole are far superior grocery stores, and a Megafoods is opening in the island's new mall. Plaza Mar, on a hill above Coxen Hill (turn up off the main Roatán road by the Bojangles), is another decent grocery store, with an Internet café as well. The **Coconut Tree Store** (tel. 504/403-8782, 7 A.M.–9:30 P.M. daily), at

the entrance to town, has a good selection of packaged food and supplies. You can find fresh produce sold from pickup trucks parked throughout West End every day except Sunday.

## OUTSIDE OF TOWN

The fanciest place in the West End, **Ooloonthoo** (tel. 504/9936-5223, 6–9 P.M. daily, reservations required), has moved just outside of town, in an elegant hilltop home off Roatán's main drag. Run by a top Canadian chef (who lived in India for three years studying the regional cuisines) and his Indian wife, the restaurant features a different chutney daily and a menu that varies with the season and the available produce. Main courses run the gamut, from coconut-citrus fish to lamb or oxtail curry. Three-course meals will set you back US$40–47.

## Services

### BANKS

Several stores and dive shops will change dollars, and most businesses accept payment in either dollars or lempiras. Take care of exchanging money in Coxen Hole if you're carrying travelers checks or another currency (like euros). There is a 24-hour **ATM** at Angelo's Gelato, but don't wait until you're down to the last dollar, as it's been known to run out of cash. There is also an ATM inside the Coconut Tree Store at the entrance to town.

### COMMUNICATIONS

The small office of **Barefoot Charlies Internet** (9 A.M.–9 P.M. daily), opposite Foster's dock, has a quick satellite connection for US$0.10 a minute, US$6 an hour, or US$10 for a two-week, unlimited time account. Headsets and mikes are also available for semi-private Skyping. The staff is very helpful on island information; T-shirts, guidebooks, and a selection of used books in many languages are also available.

Somewhat more centrally located, **Paradise Computers** (8 A.M.–10 P.M. daily) also offers Internet for US$0.10 per minute and headsets,

## ROATAN MARINE PARK RECOMMENDATIONS

The Roatan Marine Park was formed in 2005 by concerned dive operators and other local citizens, in an effort to help protect Roatán's surrounding reef. A voluntary fee of US$10 is charged to divers to help fund their protection efforts – money well spent. All visitors can also help the efforts by adhering to the following RMP suggestions:

• Use only biodegradable and nontoxic sunscreens.

• Use only eco-friendly insect repellents, especially when swimming. (DEET is highly toxic for the coral. Many stores in Roatán sell a fairly effective product called Cactus Juice, or look for Nuvy's Repelente de Insectos sold in grocery stores and pharmacies on the mainland.)

• Do not consume lobster, conch, iguana, deer,

or turtle. (All are currently endangered. We admit to eating lobster; one board member of the RMP told us the problem is the sale of lobsters whose tails are less than 5.5 inches long. Order only in reputable restaurants.)

• Recycle plastic bottles, glass, paper, and aluminum cans. Keep your use of water bottles to a minimum by refilling.

• Do not purchase marine life souvenirs. (And remember that it is illegal to leave the country with them.)

• Turn off the lights, fans, and air-conditioning when you leave your hotel room.

And for those planning to stick around Roatán for a while:

• Volunteer with the Roatan Marine Park (www.roatanmarinepark.com).

---

as well as international calls (US$0.50/minute to the United States).

### LAUNDRY
**Bamboo Hut Laundry** (8 A.M.–4 P.M. daily), just north of Georphi's hotel on the bottom floor of the owners' house, efficiently washes and dries five pounds of dirty duds for US$4, US$0.80 for each additional pound. Or, drop off your clothes at Woody's supermarket next to Posada Arco Iris Sunday–Friday, and **Hummingbird Laundry** (tel. 504/445-3154, ask for Teri or Walter) will wash it for US$0.80/pound, with a US$6.30 minimum.

### SPANISH SCHOOLS
Those interested in picking up a bit of Spanish can study at the **Roatan Language School** (tel. 504/445-4231) at the Hotel Casa Calico for US$9/hour.

### MASSAGE
If your muscles need a break from all that snorkeling, diving or beach lounging, try a massage at **Chez Breezy** (tel. 504/3313-3400,

US$50/75-minute massage) next door to Hotel Casa Calico or at **Healing Hands** (tel. 504/403-8728, US$40/60-minute massage) located at the Mariposa Lodge.

### CONSERVATION GROUPS
The offices of the **Roatan Marine Park** (tel. 504/445-4206, www.roatanmarinepark.com, 8 A.M.–6 P.M. daily) are located in the center of West End, for those interested in finding out more about where their US$10 fee is going. The office also runs the **Marine Park Green Store** on the premises, which sells T-shirts and knickknacks and rents snorkel equipment (just US$5 for 24 hours, with a US$15 deposit).

## Getting There and Around
Minibuses to and from Coxen Hole (14 kilometers) leave frequently between 7 A.M. and 7 or 8 P.M., US$1 each way. Collective taxis cost US$2. The ride to and from Sandy Bay is US$0.50 in a minibus or US$1 in a collective taxi. After dark, rides can get progressively scarcer, with the last taxis leaving toward Coxen Hole at around 10 P.M., or later on weekends.

Most taxis hang out by the highway exit by the Coconut Tree Store. After dark, hitching a lift in a passing pickup is often possible.

Water taxis to West Bay leave frequently during the day; they fill up from Foster's dock and cost US$2.50. Arrangements can be made with the captain to get picked up for the return trip later on, even after dark if you like. You can walk to West Bay along the beach in about 25 minutes, although it involves a little scamper around some wet rocks about halfway, and then crossing a tall footbridge over a canal. It can be a little treacherous at night if you don't know the way.

It's possible to buy airline tickets in Coxen Hole, or by calling the airline offices at the airport to make reservations. For the ferry, you have to go buy tickets at the dock, as they do not accept reservations. But apart from unusual circumstances (like the first boat after several days of rough seas), it's not a problem to get a seat if you show up an hour before departure. A few taxis are available early in West End to catch the ferry, but you can also speak to a taxi driver the previous day to arrange for a pickup—the drivers are usually very much in need of business and happy to get up early for the work.

## ◖ WEST BAY

Around a couple of rocky points about two kilometers south of West End is one of Roatán's greatest natural treasures—West Bay Beach, 1.5 kilometers of powdery, palm-lined sand lapped by exquisite turquoise-blue water. At the south end of the beach, where a wall of iron shore juts out into the water, the coral reef meets the shore. For anyone who wants a low-key encounter with an exceptionally fine reef without a long swim or any scuba gear, this is *the* place. It's almost too beautiful—more like an aquarium than a section of live reef, with brilliantly colored fish dodging about, the odd barracuda lurking, and sponges and sea fans gently waving—all just a few feet from the beach.

The reef comes closest to shore at the beach's south end, but for anyone willing to swim out a

bit, the entire bay is lined by excellent reef, although it's been showing the ill-effects of heavy traffic in recent years. Keep an eye out for boats when in the water. The cruise ship day-trippers frequently descend in numbers on West Bay, so it's worth checking what days the ships are coming in. Even on those days, though, the beach is generally quiet in the early morning or late afternoon, and always quieter at the northern end. Many cruise shippers end up at a section of the beach near the south end referred to as "Tabayana Beach," where beach chairs and snorkel equipment are available for rent.

Until the early 1990s, West Bay was totally deserted, save for a few bonfire-building partyers. After a sudden flurry of real-estate transactions and building, West Bay is now lined with houses and hotels, most thankfully built out of wood in a reserved, unobtrusive style.

The construction boom on West Bay and in the hills behind has brought unfortunate consequences for the nearby reef. A large wetland area a few hundred meters behind the beach, at the base of the hills, formerly served

dock at West Bay

© AMY E. ROBERTSON

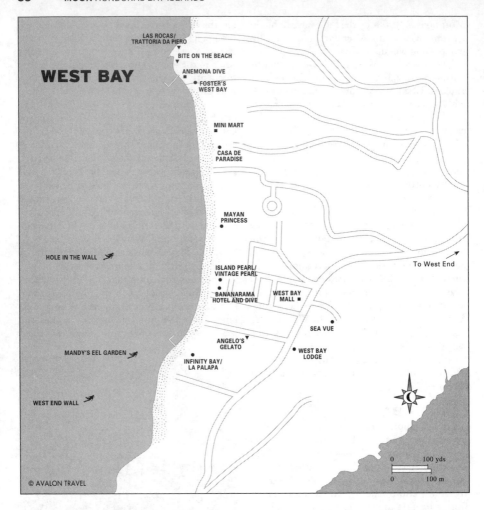

as a buffer, to catch rain runoff and either filter it or let it evaporate in the sun. Developers promptly filled in the wetlands (annoying little swamp!) when construction began in West Bay. As a result, and coupled with the hillside construction and road building, the West Bay reef is coated with waves of silty water after every strong rain. Reefs do not take well to such sudden drops in water quality, nor to the huge increase of inexperienced snorkelers and divers who bump, grab, or step on the reef, causing damage every time. The reef will still be lovely for several years to come, but it remains to be seen whether island authorities will take action to protect perhaps the single most important tourist attraction in Roatán for the future.

## Dive Shops

There are several dive shops operating out of West Bay. **Bananarama** (tel. 504/445-5005, U.S. tel. 727/564-9058, www.bananaramadive .com, fun dive US$35, beginner's Open Water certification US$325), toward the southern end of the beach, has a good reputation. **TGI** (tel. 504/403-8049, www.tgidiving.com, fun dive US$35, beginner's Open Water certification US$350) has a PADI five-star dive shop that works with the Henry Morgan and Paradise Beach Club resorts, and is scheduled to open another at Infinity Bay in September 2009. They sell equipment as well as rent. The **Mayan Princess** has its own dive shop (tel. 504/445-5050, U.S. tel. 786/299-5929, www.mayan princess.com), to which the Casa de Paradise hotel also sends its guests. At the northern end of the beach, **Las Rocas** (tel. 504/403-8046, U.S. tel. 877/379-8645, www.lasrocasresort .com) has a dive shop, and **Anemona** (tel. 504/3266-6719, www.anemonadivers.com) is run out of Foster's hotel. All of the shops have package deals available with their affiliated hotel.

## Snorkeling

One of the main attractions of West Bay is the reef located right offshore, easily accessible to even the most novice snorkeler. At the southern end of the beach, the reef is just a few meters offshore, while reaching the reef from the northern end of the beach requires a long swim, which should be done with a companion for safety. Tropical fish and colorful coral abound. Stay attuned to the buzzing sound of the occasional water taxi.

*Note:* Snorkelers must take care to avoid touching the reef at all. The thousands of visitors every month who descend upon West Bay's reef are taking a heavy toll. It may be easy for novice snorkelers to enjoy the reef, but it's also easy for them to bump into or actually step on the coral.

## Other Recreation

If you came to Roatán with family and your child is too little to snorkel, or someone isn't able, a trip on the **glass-bottom boat** (US$30 adults, US$15 kids) that moors at the dock near Foster's is a good, albeit pricey, way to see a few of those fish that everyone else is talking about.

---

# SNORKELING

Many of us land-based creatures feel slightly ill at ease strapping on all that scuba gear and descending to the watery depths. We would much prefer to admire the undersea world wearing nothing more complicated than a mask, a snorkel, and fins. Snorkel gear is easily rented at any dive shop on the islands. When renting gear, be very careful to check that your mask fits snugly. Hold the mask against your face and suck in with your nose – it should stay held against your face without the help of your hand. Also, see that the snorkel has no obvious leaks (some shops are more conscientious than others) and fits in your mouth comfortably, and that your fins are neither too tight nor too loose. A constantly dripping mask or a painfully tight fin can ruin a good snorkel trip. Bringing your own mask is one way to avoid this problem. A good fit for the fins is important also.

On all the Bay Islands, snorkelers will find several good locations to paddle out to from shore. But more adventurous snorkelers, who are also confident swimmers, can often go out with scuba boats and snorkel the same site as the divers, but from above. Ask around at different shops for appropriate dive sites, preferably shallow ones.

---

Somewhat corny, but fun nevertheless, is **Gumbalimba Park** (tel./fax 504/9914-9196 or 504/9946-5559, www.gumbalimbapark .com, 7 A.M.–5 P.M. daily, US$20), a little natural oasis in West Bay complete with a waterfall, cactus garden, 100-plus species of orchids, 25 species of heliconia, and—the part that makes it worth a trip—a parrot, macaw, and monkey park where the trained animals roam and fly free. The animals are best viewed between 8 A.M. and 3 P.M. Be prepared to have any or all of the three tropical critters take perch on your shoulder. Guides are included in the price, as is transportation—be sure to take advantage of both (the guides will make sure you go home

© LUCA RENDA

building sand castles on West Bay Beach

with that shot of a parrot or monkey on your shoulder). The park also runs canopy tours.

The park, on the land of the owner of Anthony's Key Resort, has an assortment of attractions catering generally to the cruise-ship crowd, but available to others also, including a beach with snorkeling, clear kayaks for rent (to see the reef below), horseback riding in the park (US$35 for 1.5 hours). Snacks and meals are served at an outdoor restaurant. It can be pretty busy when the cruise ships are in town, or extremely quiet when they are not.

Also located along the road between West Bay and West End is **South Shore Canopy** (tel. 504/9967-1381, US$45).

For a different way to see the beach, or a bit of the jungle if desired, contact **Barrio Dorcas Ranch** (tel. 504/9555-4880, www.barriodorcasranch.com), for a tour by horseback (US$35–40).

If all these activities have left your muscles aching, look for one of the impromptu massage shops that spring up on the beach when the cruise ships are in town, typically charging US$20 for a 30-minute massage.

One of the best places to arrange any activity is at the two **Roatan Tourist Info Centers**

(www.roatantouristinfo.com, tel. 504/3336-5597) located near Foster's and Bananarama. They offer tickets to Gumbalimba and for the glass-bottom boat, book catamaran sail and snorkel tours of Roatán (US$35), and can arrange activities around the island, such as a visit to the pirate canopy tour and iguana farm near French Harbour, Jet-Skiing in Flowers Bay, kayak rentals at West Bay, car rentals, and so forth. Surprisingly, prices are usually the same as you pay if you purchase services directly, or slightly more but transportation is included (a big perk).

## Accommodations

Hotels in West Bay are a decided step up in price from West End, although there are still many reasonable options by international standards. Those who are really after some peace and quiet, and some serious beach time, may enjoy staying in West Bay. And while the restaurant selection can't compete with West End, there are several spots worth seeking out. Some rooms in West Bay also have kitchens, or at least mini-fridges and microwaves, which can be useful for breakfasts and snacks.

Rates skyrocket from those listed here during

Easter and Christmas weeks, when rooms should be booked well in advance. Remember, all room rates are subject to a 16 percent tax, which has been included here but may or may not be included in the price quoted to you by the establishment itself. **Foster's West Bay** (tel. 504/445-1124, U.S. tel. 877/245-5907, www.fostersroatan.com, US$64–81 d, US$87–162 for suites, cabins, and duplexes that sleep 2–5) owns several cabins near the north end of West Bay beach. In addition, a small room built into the branches of a mango tree, complete with electricity and running water, rents for US$64–104 d, depending on the season. One-, two-, and three-bedroom units are also available.

One of the giants in West Bay is **Hotel Mayan Princess** (tel. 504/445-5050, U.S. tel. 786/299-5929, www.mayanprincess.com, US$211–277, with discounts during the low season and weekly rates available), a collection of plaster-and-tile units along the beach equipped with comfortable wicker furniture, satellite TV, telephones, master bedrooms, sofa beds, and kitchens. "Suites" have two bedrooms and rent for US$319–520. The units are all privately owned, and then rented out by hotel management when the owners are not using them. Price includes transportation to and from the airport. The hotel's restaurant/bar is open 7:30 A.M.–10 P.M. daily, although there are better places to eat on the beach.

The newest addition to West Bay's collection of large and luxurious hotels is **( Infinity Bay** (tel. 504/445-5016, U.S. tel. 866/369-1977, www.infinitybay.com), located at the southern end of West Bay, close to where the reef reaches the shore. Although construction was still going on at the time of writing, the first-phase units have been completed and were available for rent (US$162–197 studio, US$231–307 one bedroom, US$242–423 two bedroom, US$481–539 3 bedroom). The massive complex will have 145 rooms upon completion, the largest hotel on West Bay. Rooms have beautiful furnishings, patios or balconies, and amenities such as large flat-screen TVs. All but the studios have full kitchens, and many have sofa-beds for additional capacity. A long swimming pool runs down the center of the complex, leading to the bar on the beach. What's noteworthy about this resort is its significant efforts to have zero negative impacts on Roatán's beach and reef. Environmentally friendly aspects include state-of-the-art water treatment and septic facilities, solar water heating, the use of biodegradable soaps in housekeeping, and an awareness of erosion control in the construction process. The only drawback we found (besides, perhaps, its behemoth size), was that the windows for ground-floor units open onto walkways, limiting privacy for those who like to keep the curtains drawn.

A relatively budget choice on West Bay is **Bananarama** (tel. 504/445-5005, U.S. tel. 727/564-9058, www.bananaramadive.com, US$94–123 d, with specials available in the low season). A variety of simple but decent garden and beach-front rooms can sleep up to five, although there is a US$10 per person charge for more than two guests. There is also a two-bedroom house that can sleep up to 12, priced at US$350 for double occupancy. Cruise ship excursions are offered through Bananarama, so it can get fairly chaotic some days, but the on-site dive shop has a good reputation and fair prices.

Bananarama recently purchased the neighboring property, **( Island Pearl** (tel. 504/445-5005, U.S. tel. 727/564-9058, www.roatanpearl.com), but seems to be maintaining it as a quieter, more upscale accommodation, although the unique artwork left with the previous owners. The attractive apartments in four separate houses set among shady trees rent for US$232–290, and a studio with queen bed is available for US$116. Accommodations for 3–5 guests are available for an additional US$10 per person. The on-site restaurant, Vintage Pearl, is very highly regarded.

An Italian conglomerate (tel. 504/445-5009, www.hmresorts.com) is the owner of several all-inclusive hotels on West Bay, including **Henry Morgan Resort, Paradise Beach Club,** and **Las Sirenas.** The first is especially renowned for its throngs of Italian package tourists. Paradise Beach Club has lovely grounds, with winding paths and lush tropical foliage leading between the buildings and around the swimming pool. Guests have reported being disappointed by the somewhat simple rooms given the price. For rates and information, call tel. 504/445-5009 or check www.hmresorts.com.

**Casa de Paradise** (tel. 504/9961-5311, U.S. tel. 740/251-4123, www.casadeparadise.com) is actually two *casas* (houses), with five different accommodations ranging from a one-bedroom efficiency suite to a deluxe four-bedroom home. Amenities vary by room but may include a king bed, TV, hammock, balcony, or full kitchen. All rooms come with coffee from owners Ron and Myra Cummin's plantation in Olancho. Prices range US$92–327; monthly rates are also available. Unusual in this price range, air-conditioning is charged separately (US$12 per unit used per day). Thankfully the hotel's small size hasn't kept it from getting a generator to keep the air-conditioning running during the occasional power outage. Casa de Paradise works with the well-regarded dive shop at the nearby Hotel Mayan Princess.

**Las Rocas** (tel. 504/403-8046, U.S. tel. 877/379-8645, www.lasrocasresort.com) has several two-story wood cabins tucked along its own private beach, two minutes along a wooden boardwalk from West Bay proper. Rooms are named after Italian islands such as Capri and Stromboli, thanks to its Italian-expat owner, Piero. The best rooms are the "superior" (US$103–151), which are spacious and tasteful, with wood furniture and floors, and peaked ceilings. Standard rooms (US$80–127) lack water views but are just as spacious and have porches with hammocks, while the "value" rooms (US$75–110) are smaller and in cabins built claustrophobically close together. The resort has its own dive shop, and dive packages are available, a good deal at US$532–730 per week, based on double occupancy.

Set back from the beach a few hundred meters (opposite the West Bay Mall) is **Sea Vue** (tel. 504/445-5002, www.seavueroatan.com, US$75–133 for up to four people), with four very attractive condos, each with a full kitchen, and two bedrooms that can sleep up to six. High ceilings, white walls, and a sleek design give the place an airy, bright feel, and all units have an ocean view. There is an outdoor swimming pool and Jacuzzi, and an ecologically friendly water collection and disposal system for the hotel. A path next to the West Bay Mall leads to the beach, a four- or five-minute walk away. This is a great deal for anyone who doesn't mind the walk. Cars are available for rent from the owners as well.

Another option nearby (that is, also a four-minute walk from the beach) is **West Bay Lodge** (tel. 504/445-5069, U.S. tel. 503/761-7172, www.westbaylodge.com, US$93–145 d), with cute little bungalows tucked into tropical gardens, each with its own porch and hammock. "Supreme" units with kitchens and two double beds are available for US$25–30 more. There is a pool on-site, perfect for cooling off after the beach, and guests rave about the breakfasts.

*Note:* In December 2008 there were two evening muggings on this path that leads between the beach and West Bay Mall—highly unusual according to local police, but be attentive to your surroundings after dark.

## Food and Entertainment

Located on the wooden walkway between Foster's and Las Rocas is **Bite on the Beach** (noon–9 P.M. Tues.–Sat., with extended hours for the bar), a superb spot to enjoy a snack, beer, or full meal on a large, breezy deck right on the edge of the glorious Caribbean. The standard fish, shrimp, lobster, and chicken are available in various preparations, as well as more unusual dishes such as *caprese* salad and Thai curries, for US$5.50–15 per plate. If you've been fishing, they'll even cook up your own catch of the day.

**Foster's West Bay** (8 A.M.–9 P.M. daily), at the north end of West Bay shortly before Bite on the Beach, serves tasty breakfasts, seafood entrées (US$8–15), and sandwiches (US$5–8) prepared at an open-air *champa*, or thatched hut. The coconut bread French toast and the grilled lobster (just US$12 on Thursdays) are especially recommended. The bar/restaurant is a popular hangout spot with locals and foreigners alike during the lazy afternoons at West Bay.

**(** **Vintage Pearl** is an excellent, upscale restaurant. While the menu selection is limited, every plate is good. The prix-fixe menu changes daily and runs US$25–50 for the three courses. The restaurant has the largest wine cellar on the island. A great place for a romantic splurge.

**Trattoria da Piero,** at Las Rocas Resort, has good Caribbean food with an Italian twist, thanks to hotel owner Piero. Fresh seafood is of course the specialty, and the shrimp in pesto sauce and seafood risotto are great ways to shake off the monotony of beach cuisine. There is even pasta in meat sauce for those really looking for something different (mains US$16–23).

Set under the palm trees on the sand, Infinity Bay's restaurant **La Palapa** serves up good breakfasts, burgers, and fish sandwiches (US$4–9), as well as fancier dishes like Thai curry, grilled lobster, and filet mignon (US$12–23).

**Mangiamo Market and Deli** (8:30 A.M.–5 P.M. Mon.–Sat.), in the West Bay Mall, makes excellent sandwiches, including prosciutto with mozzarella, a spicy chipotle chicken, and good ole turkey for US$7–9, perfect for a picnic on the beach. Breakfasts are available too, for take-away or to munch at one of the deli's small tables.

## Services

The **Mini-Mart** (8 A.M.–9 P.M. daily, on the beach between Foster's and Henry Morgan) has basic supplies such as Panadol (a good substitute for Tylenol) and pasta, as well as Internet access for US$0.10 per minute.

The petite **West Bay Mall** has a number of handy shops—to get there, follow the path that's between Bananarama and Paradise Beach Club out to the road, and the mall is just to the left. Those looking to stock up on their own supplies can find a nice variety of high-quality goods at

Impromptu massage parlors look out toward the water from West Bay Beach.

**Mangiamo Market and Deli** (8:30 A.M.–5 P.M. Mon.–Sat.), such as gourmet chocolate, granola bars, beer, and ingredients for pasta. There is a branch of **Captain Van's Rentals** (tel. 504/445-5040, 9 A.M.–7 P.M. daily) here, renting scooters, motorcycles, mountain bikes, cell phones, and DVDs. Stock up on wine, cigars, and rum at **De la Viña** (10 A.M.–7 P.M. Mon.–Thurs., 11 A.M.–7 P.M. Fri.). Lastly, the mall also houses **Cool Beans** (tel. 504/445-5048, 7:30 A.M.–5 P.M. Mon.–Fri., 8 A.M.–noon Sat.–Sun.), a nice coffee house with bagels and tasty cakes.

There is an **Internet** shop just across the road from the mall.

## Getting There

From West End, you can walk to West Bay (45 minutes along the beach, past the rickety wooden dock on the point—do not carry valuables as there has been the occasional mugging along this route), or take a water taxi (US$2.50 from Foster's) or car (a four-kilometer paved road turns off the main highway near the entrance to West End, while another paved road connects Coxen Hole to West Bay via Flowers

Bay). Water-taxi captains are happy to arrange a return trip to pick up weary but content sun-fried beach bums at the end of the day.

## Near West Bay

Along the road from West Bay to West End, just before reaching the latter, is **Luna Beach Resort** (tel. 504/403-8778, U.S. tel. 866/710-5862, www.lunabeachresort.com, US$89–246 s/d, US$25 each extra person), an expanse of wooden buildings and decks spread across the beach and up a hillside between West End and West Bay. It has a fine dock out over the water, perfect for swimming, sunbathing, and watching the sunset, as well as a pool and beachfront bar. A hotel-style portion has spacious rooms along the waterfront, while upscale cabins with kitchens and generous living areas are nestled into the tropical hillside. The furniture is made with local wood, the beach is very well-maintained, including a daily spraying with a natural *jején* repellent, and the amenities (showers, TVs, appliances) are all first-class—pluses that make up for a lack of character in the decor. Enormous four-bedroom houses are available for $408/night. There is a dive shop on-site with competitive prices (fun dive US$35, Open Water certification US$325 for beginners, US$260 for advanced), and the confined sessions can be completed in the hotel pool, a luxury if the sea is choppy.

## SANDY BAY

With a full-time population of about 1,200, Sandy Bay is considerably larger than West End, but somehow it doesn't feel like it. The town is a collection of weather-beaten wooden houses, most built on stilts among patches of shady trees a hundred meters or so from the edge of the sea, strung out over three or more kilometers of shoreline. Development has arrived in Sandy Bay, but it's mostly limited to private houses and a couple of low-key resorts tucked away in the corners of town. Anthony's Key Resort (AKR), which literally divides Sandy Bay in two, is a large complex, but most guests don't venture off the grounds into town, so it doesn't much disturb the placid lifestyle of the local islanders. Sandy Bay is a popular place for foreigners living in Roatán to rent inexpensive houses or apartments.

## Sights

In one of the few programs of its kind in the Caribbean, **The Institute for Marine Sciences** based at AKR studies the local dolphin population and runs a variety of highly regarded interactions with them. Spectators are welcome to stop by daily at 4 P.M. for the informal dolphin show (call first to confirm the time, as it can vary), where trainers work with the dolphins and perform health checks. Certified scuba divers can enjoy 45 minutes of controlled but unstructured swimming with dolphins over open-water sand flats (US$112, extra to rent equipment). You can also snorkel for 30 minutes with the dolphins for US$84, or have a beachside "dolphin encounter" for US$60, complete with a dolphin kiss. An institute trainer accompanies all diving and snorkeling expeditions. Those interested in more detailed information on the dolphins can take a specialty course, with one day of lessons and activities (US$160 pp for AKR guests, or US$202 for nonguests). Information about the institute and the dolphin activities is available on AKR's website, www.anthonyskey.com.

The IMS has several exhibits on invertebrates, reptiles, birds, fish, coral-reef life, and the geology of the Bay Islands, as well as a small but worthwhile bilingual museum on local archaeology and history. Admission to the institute's museum is US$2; the facility is open 8 A.M.–5 P.M. daily.

**Carambola Botanical Gardens** (tel. 504/445-3117, www.carambolagardens.com, 8 A.M.–5 P.M. daily, US$5, age seven and under free), located off the highway opposite the entrance to AKR, is the only developed inland reserve on the Bay Islands. Well-built trails wind through forests of ferns, spices, orchids, flowering plants, fruit trees, and even a few mahogany trees. A decidedly steep trail leads to the top of Carambola Mountain. Along the way is a turnoff to the fascinating Iguana Wall, a section of sheer cliff that serves as a protected breeding ground for iguanas and parrots. There are great views from the peak over the surrounding reef and, in the distance, Utila. The staff at the visitors center has some information on the reserves, and if manager Irma Brady is around, she is particularly knowledgeable about the reserve's flora and fauna. Guides can be hired for an extra charge.

## Recreation

As its name would suggest, Sandy Bay has plenty of beach right in front of town, but the water is somewhat muddy and not totally clean, making it not as nice for sunbathing as West End or West Bay. The waters around Sandy Bay and AKR were the first established section of the Roatan Marine Park, created in 1989, and the snorkeling and diving are superb. Snorkelers can paddle out anywhere that's convenient across a couple hundred meters of shallow water, much of it blanketed in sea grass, to the edge of the reef. Finding a passage out across the shallow reef can be tricky—the best plan is to ask locals to point out the channels used by boats, marked by buoys. The steep coral and rock cliffs and formations on the ocean side of the reef are dramatic and great fun to explore with a snorkel and fins. When swimming, keep a sharp eye out for boat traffic.

The dive shops at AKR and Blue Bahia will take nonguest divers, for slightly higher rates than at West End. Most West End shops will set up trips out to Sandy Bay dive sites on request.

## Accommodations

Sandy Bay's hotel selection tends to the middle and upper price categories. It's often possible to find a local in the many wooden houses lining the beach happy to rent out a room or an entire cabin for a negotiable fee.

Run by Bill and Cathy Service, **Sunnyside Condominiums** (tel./fax 504/445-3006, www .sunnysideroatan.com, US$50–200/night, US$500–1,400/week), on the beach at the eastern end of Sandy Bay, has rental options including two studio apartments, a condo, and two large houses, and priced for a couple on up to a group or family of six or more.

The **Roatan Beachcomber** (tel. 504/9929-

4720, www.roatanbeachcomber.com) also has a variety of accommodations, right on the beach. Two apartments are available for those who want their own kitchen (US$58–75 one bedroom, US$116–145 two bedroom), adjacent to the restaurant. There is a large wooden building on stilts that looks out over the water, and its simple cabin-style rooms have peek-a-boo ocean views; they are a great value at US$35–58 (the high end of the range for a/c). Each has a double bed, and mattresses can be brought in for kids. If a group rents several rooms, they can also request use of the common kitchen (off-limits to individual travelers). Lastly, there is a four-bedroom beach house available for US$992–1,334 per week. While none of the digs are particularly fancy, the managers take exceptional care of the beach (our visit was post-storm when no one else was managing to keep the driftwood and seaweed off the shore, yet here the sand had been fastidiously raked), and the reef is a very short swim from the hotel's private dock. Snorkeling equipment is provided, kayaks are available for rent on-site, and fishing charters and diving trips can be arranged. There is a restaurant on-site.

Still a bit up-and-coming is **Tranquil Seas** (tel. 504/445-3351, www.tranquilseas.co.uk, US$122 s/d), with a handful of lovely cabins in a lush tropical setting. The rooms are tastefully decorated, and a few have kitchenettes. An attractive thatch-roof restaurant and bar overlooks the small but nice swimming pool. New cabins are still under construction, however, so until those are finished, the place might not be quite as peaceful as you hoped. Customer service is normally reputed to be stellar, but it seems to fall apart when the owner heads back to his native U.K. for summer vacation. There are plans to put a dive shop on-site, but for now guests can head a few steps down the beach to the Octopus dive shop at the Blue Bahia Resort. This will be a great place to stay when the kinks are worked out.

Roatán's most extravagant option, **Mayoka Lodge** (tel. 504/445-3043, www.mayokalodge .com), is on two hectares of tropical gardens near town. The six-suite lodge has a swimming pool, tennis court, and two holes of golf, as well as luxuries such as a wine cellar, chef, car and driver, and, of course, your own private beach and dock. It's all yours for a mere US$22,500 per week.

Just off the southern side of the highway, the **Oasis Lounge** restaurant (www.roatan-guava-grove.com, US$41/day or US$580/month) also rents efficiency suites, suitable for those with their own wheels to get to the beach. There is also a three-bedroom house for rent with a water view over the treetops (US$174/night or US$986/week). The lounge/restaurant is closed on Wednesdays.

## Dive Resorts

One of the premier vacation resorts on Roatán and, for that matter, in all of Honduras, ◖ **Anthony's Key Resort** (AKR, tel. 504/445-3003, U.S. tel. 800/227-3483, www .anthonyskey.com, US$973–1,832 pp for one-week dive packages) manages 56 cabins on both the small and serene Anthony's Key and on a tree-covered hillside on the mainland of Roatán. "Leisure" packages are room-

only and run US$683–1,460 per person for a week, or US$108–230 per person per night. There's fantastic swimming and snorkeling on all sides and a small sunbathing beach as well as a new pool and poolside bar on the cay. Dive shop facilities are top-notch, with several large boats, new equipment, and everything needed for a variety of PADI courses. The resort is renowned for its dolphin encounter and educational programs. AKR has its own underwater photo/video shop, offering dive light rentals, film and batteries for sale, underwater videos, and pictures from the dolphin encounter and dolphin dives.

A few minutes down the road, but just steps away via the beach, is the **Blue Bahia Resort** (tel. 504/445-3385, www.bluebahiaresort .com, US$115–215 depending on room size, and a 50 percent discount Sept.–Nov.), with nine lovely rooms set around an infinity-edged pool that looks out toward the water. Each has a sitting area and porch with deck chairs, and several have full kitchens as well, although given the quality of the resort's restaurant, the only meal you may find yourself

dolphins performing at Anthony's Key Resort, in Sandy Bay

© AMY E. ROBERTSON

making is breakfast (when the resort restaurant is closed). The beach is not bad, but doesn't compare to West Bay or some of the others; the hotel is best suited to those who have come to Roatán to dive. The **Octopus Dive School** (tel. 504/9737-9120, www.roatan-octopus diveschool.com) is on-site, offering the standard PADI Open Water course for US$325, specialty courses such as Nitrox (US$220), and half-day introductions to scuba for adults (US$60) and children (US$75, ages eight and up). Fun dives are US$25–35).

Located at Gibson Bight, the **Inn of Last Resort** (tel. 504/445-4113, U.S. tel. 888/319-3255, www.innoflastresort.com) offers week-long dive packages for US$806–1,270 per person per week and has rates available for shorter stays and non-divers as well. The resort is located on a small lagoon that opens out to the ocean, and its dive boats and equipment were all new in early 2009.

## Food and Entertainment

Those staying in Sandy Bay will likely be eating in their resort restaurant, but a couple of other places serve good meals at midrange prices.

Even if you're not staying at the Blue Bahia Resort, its restaurant is well worth a visit. The ◖ **Beach Grill** (open for lunch and dinner every day but Tuesday) smokes its own meats and is renowned for its Louisiana-style barbecue, including brisket, chicken and ribs, as well as pulled-pork sandwiches, the latter served on house-baked bread (US$8–13).

The **Blue Parrot Bar and Restaurant** (tel. 504/992-2807, 11:30 A.M.–10 P.M. Mon.–Sat.) is a nice little street-front joint with a colorful parrot mural on the wall. The owner has recently changed, but locals say it's as good as ever, with sandwiches for around US$5 and entrées like lobster, shrimp kebabs, and surf 'n' turf for US$7–12 a meal.

The **Sunshine Café** at the Roatan Beachcomber is open noon–9 P.M. daily; its specialty is a Friday night all-you-can-eat fish fry with shrimp, conch, and fish for US$15.

The Bay Island Beach Resort hosts crab races at **Deep Ted's Grille** on Thursday evenings,

complete with a pig roast and plenty of tequila. It's a popular event with the local expat community, and proceeds are donated to the Sandy Bay public schools.

The multi-service **Oasis Lounge** (just off the southern side of the highway) has American-friendly snacks such as wings and burgers, as well as more upscale *tapas* and salads, all served in a lounge tented by billowy fabrics. There are nightly activities popular with Roatán expats, such as a pub quiz (Tuesdays) and movies (Thursdays), as well as a swimming pool (with a kids' swim Fridays noon–5 P.M.). There are also efficiency suites and a house for rent (www.roatan-guavagrove.com). The lounge/restaurant is closed on Wednesdays.

## Spas

Undoubtedly the finest spa on the island, **Baan Suerte** (tel. 504/445-3059, www.spa baansuerte.com) is tucked into lush vegetation on a hill above the sea, offering five types of massage, seven body treatments (such honey and papaya, or green tea-mint-algae), and other spa standards like facials, manicures, and yoga. Services are expensive (massages and body treatments run US$70–150), but quality is top-notch, and guests are welcome to stay as long as they like on the property, taking advantage of the swimming pool, beach access, kayaks, and snorkel equipment.

## Services

On the grounds of AKR is the **Cornerstone Medical Center** (tel. 504/445-3003 or 504/445-3049, VHF channel 16, 8 A.M.–5 P.M. daily, 24 hours for diving emergencies), home to one of the two recompression tanks on Roatán (the other is at Fantasy Island Resort). It has X-ray facilities, and the doctors can treat ailments resulting from diving and other illnesses as well.

For non-diving injuries and illnesses, head to the **Clínica Esperanza** (tel. 504/445-3234), just off the highway, for perhaps the best health care on the island. The drawback? Would-be patients must arrive between 7 and 9 A.M. to take a number, then wait around until called.

Sandy Bay is just off the West End–Coxen Hole highway; minibuses and taxis pass frequently in both directions. Shared taxis to Coxen Hole cost US$1.50; it's US$1 to West End.

## COXEN HOLE

A dusty, unremarkable town of weather-beaten wooden houses and shops, Coxen Hole is visited most frequently to change money, buy groceries, or take care of other business. All buses across the island are based out of Coxen Hole, and the airport is three kilometers east of town, on the road to French Harbour.

Named for pirate captain John Coxen, who lived on Roatán from 1687 to 1697, the town was founded in 1835, when several families arrived from the Cayman Islands and settled on the harbor.

### Shopping

**Yaba Ding Ding** (tel. 504/445-1683, 9 A.M.–5 P.M. Mon.–Sat.)—which is the islanders' nickname for pre-Columbian artifacts—carries paintings by well-known Honduran painters like Virginia Castillo, carvings, batik, woven *junco* baskets from Santa Bárbara, Honduran and Cuban cigars, T-shirts, and more. It's one of the best handicraft stores on the island, and well worth a visit if you happen to be wandering through Coxen Hole. The store is on the ground floor of a two-story building next to H.B. Warren's supermarket.

In the center of town (to the left, or east, when arriving into town along the main road from the highway) is **H.B. Warren's** (7 A.M.–6 P.M. Mon.–Sat.), one of the best supermarkets on the island (along with Eldon's in French Harbour, and a Megafoods in the new mall will soon give everyone a run for their money).

### Accommodations

Though most sun- and sand-seekers proceed directly from the docks and airport to West End, Sandy Bay, or elsewhere, there are a handful of hotels in Coxen Hole should you need to spend the night there for some reason.

The **Hotel Cay View** (tel. 504/445-1202, US$31 s, US$38 d), on the eastern side of town on Main Street, has some quite decent rooms that have recently been remodeled, a couple of which even have water views, with air-conditioning, TV, and hot water. The older rooms are pretty dingy.

If the Cay View is full, an alternative is the **Hotel Bella Vista** (tel. 504/445-3611, US$35 d).

### Food and Entertainment

While there aren't any standout restaurants in Coxen Hole proper, there are plenty of places to try Honduran staples such as *baleadas,* fluffy flour tortillas stuffed with refried beans and a dash of sour cream, and roast chicken; just walk along Coxen Hole's main drag and pop into one that appeals to you.

### Banks

Most of the banks in town are on Main Street (the road that runs along the water) and are open Monday–Friday from 8:30 A.M. until 3:30 or 4 P.M., Saturday from 8:30 A.M. until 11 or 11:30 A.M.

**Banco Atlántida** (tel. 504/445-1225) has a cash machine, linked only to the Visa network. It will advance lempiras on a Visa card, though at a poor exchange rate, and exchange a maximum of US$300 travelers checks. **HSBC** exchanges unlimited amounts of dollars and travelers checks and offers Visa cash advances at a reasonable exchange rate. It also has an ATM, linked to the Plus, Unibanc, and Visa networks. MoneyGrams can be picked up here. **BAC Bamer** (tel. 504/445-1703) offers cash advances on Visa, American Express, and MasterCard, but the exchange rate is not the best. Its cash machine is linked to the Cirrus, Unibanc, and Plus networks.

Be forewarned that the lines to exchange travelers checks can be horrendously long.

### Communications

**Honducor** is in the small square in the center of town. Across the street from Wood Medical Center is **Hondutel** (fax 504/445-1206, 8 A.M.–noon and 12:30–4 P.M. Mon.–Fri.).

**Paradise Computers** (tel. 504/445-1394,

www.paradise-computers.com), in the Mango Tree Center on the highway headed to Sandy Bay, has Internet access for US$0.10 per minute, and international calls can be made from here (US$0.50/minute for calls to the United States). It has a small Internet and call center on the cruise ship dock as well.

**Martinez Cyber Center** (tel. 504/445-1432, 8 A.M.–10 P.M. Mon.–Sat.), in the center of town, has Internet connections for US$0.10 a minute or US$2 per hour. It also offers great rates on international calls (US$0.05 a minute to the United States). The shop is along Main Street, not far from H.B. Warren, but on the opposite side of the street.

### Emergencies

In case of emergency, call the **police** (tel. 504/445-3438); the main police station on the island is outside of Coxen Hole on the highway toward West End, on the left-hand side about a kilometer outside of town.

For the **fire department** the number is 504/445-0430.

**Pharmacy Roatan** (tel. 504/445-1260, 9 A.M.–6 P.M. Mon.–Fri., 9 A.M.–2 P.M. Sat.) is on the road leading to the West End highway from downtown.

**Wood Medical Center** (tel. 504/445-1080) opposite Cay View is not the finest operation in existence, but it does have one of the few X-ray machines on the island.

### Immigration

On the small square in the center of town are the *migración* office (tel. 504/445-1326) and the **port captain** (8 A.M.–noon and 2–5 P.M. Mon.–Fri., 8 A.M.–noon Sat.).

### Getting There and Away

**Office Mart** (tel. 504/445-1843), at Welcome's Plaza (at the juncture of Main Street and Thickett Road), can book airline tickets with **Sosa** airlines.

For most visitors, collective taxis or minibuses are the best way to move between Coxen Hole and other parts of the island. Collective taxis gather in front of H.B. Warren's to pick up passengers to West End (US$1.50), Sandy Bay (US$1), Brick Bay (US$1.50), French Harbour (US$1.50), and Oak Ridge (US$2.25). Minibuses cost less than half what taxis charge. Private taxi rides are negotiable (always negotiate before getting in) and usually expensive, especially for foreign tourists.

## FLOWERS BAY

The main ocean road heading north from Coxen Hole leads to the small town of Flowers Bay, home to the island's most popular late-night spot, **Hip Hop**. Despite the name, country-western music is the number one rhythm of choice, and the place gets going promptly at 2:15 A.M., when everything else on the island has closed and those in the know start to show up here.

## FRENCH HARBOUR AND VICINITY

A large south-coast town set about one kilometer off the highway on a wide peninsula 10 kilometers east of Coxen Hole, French Harbour is home to one of the island's two major fishing fleets (the other is based in Oak Ridge). This is a working town, and while watching the activity on the docks is interesting, French Harbour is not particularly visually attractive. Nevertheless, the town has a cheerful character that Coxen Hole lacks. There isn't much of a beach or dive-worthy reef around French Harbour—it's better to go farther east or west up the coast.

French Harbour is thought to be named for a Frenchman who had one of the first homesteads in the area during the British military occupation in the 1740s.

### Accommodations

The best option in town is **Casa Romeo's** (tel. 504/455-5854, www.casaromeos.com, US$65 s, US$87 d, with discounts available in the low season), a large, stylish wooden house built on the dock, with a cool and quiet restaurant downstairs serving excellent seafood (the prices reflect the quality). The seven rooms are a tiny bit worn, but bright, whitewashed, and breezy with wood floors, air-conditioning, fans, and harbor views. Dive and meal packages are available, and rates come down for weeklong stays.

Upstairs from Gio's restaurant and run by the same owners is **The Faro Inn** (tel. 504/445-5214, US$52 s, US$58 d), with seven decent rooms each with cable TV, air-conditioning, and hot water but, at the time of our visit, decidedly unfriendly staff.

A few kilometers outside of town toward Coxen Hole is the lavish **Barefoot Cay** (tel. 504/455-6235, U.S. tel. 866/246-3706, www.barefootcay.com), located on its own private 1.6-hectare cay (island) 100 meters off Roatán's mainland. Rooms are modern and elegant, with tile floors, Balinese showers, wood furnishings, and white linens set off by colorful pillows. Rooms, suites, and villas rent for US$155–395 per person; weekly rates and all-inclusive packages (with or without diving) are also available. There is yacht moorage and a dive shop on site, as well as a beautiful outdoor pool. The dive shop (www.barefootdiversroatan.com) is pricier than those in West End or West Bay, charging US$40 for a fun dive and US$450 for the beginner's Open Water certification.

Five kilometers from town the other direction (toward Oak Ridge) is **Santé Wellness Center** (tel. 504/408-5156, U.S. tel. 510/455-4232, www.santewellnesscenter.com, US$168–191 d), a quiet hotel on its own cay in front of the large Parrot Tree Plantation. With just three guest rooms and owners that live on-site, everything at Santé benefits from a personal touch. Great snorkeling is available right from the beach, and there is a swimming pool for anyone who tires of the saltwater. Meals are fresh and spa-healthy, complementing the extensive list of spa services.

## Food and Entertainment

Famed for its legendary king crab *al ajillo* (cooked in garlic), **Gio's** (tel. 504/455-5214, 9 A.M.–2 P.M. and 5–10 P.M. Mon.–Sat.), set out over the water, also serves fish, shrimp, several kinds of pasta, and a decent cut of beef at US$8–26 an entrée.

Owned by Italian-Honduran Romeo Silvestri, **Casa Romeo's** (tel. 504/455-5854, www.casaromeos.com, 10 A.M.–2:30 P.M. and 5–10 P.M. Mon.–Sat.), just up the street, has plenty of pastas as well as superb seafood, such as conch chowder, king crab, and the "AKR Special" (squid, shrimp, lobster, and snapper), at US$7–23 per entrée, served in a classy dining room on the edge of the harbor. To reach the restaurant, enter French Harbour from the main road, pass the police station and take the right fork, go over a little bridge, and you will see Romeo's a little farther on the right of the road (Gio's is just a little bit farther down the road).

**Eldon's,** at the French Harbour turnoff, is considered by some to be the best supermarket on the island and certainly has the best fresh vegetables (7 A.M.–7 P.M. Mon.–Fri., 7 A.M.–8 P.M. Sat., 8 A.M.–1 P.M. Sun.).

People come from all over the island to **H2O** (tel. 504/455-7552, open Thurs.–Sun.), a dance club outside of town.

## Services

**BAC Bamer** just past Casa Romeo's on the left, will exchange U.S. dollars and travelers checks, as well as advance cash on a Visa card. Farther down the road, near Gio's, is **Banffaa,** exchanging dollars and travelers checks.

If you're looking to get online, head to the **Gone Bananas Kafe** in the McNab Plaza at the main road at the eastern end of town.

The Coxen Hole–Oak Ridge buses, which run until late afternoon, pull all the way into town, so there's no need to slog out to the highway. The fare to Coxen Hole is US$0.80. A collective taxi to Coxen Hole costs US$1.50.

The French Harbour **police station** is on the main road, up from the harbor near the bus station (tel. 504/455-5099).

## Palmetto Bay

A magnificently isolated beach resort on the north side of Roatán, **Palmetto Bay Plantation** (tel. 504/445-5702 or 504/991-0811, www.palmettobayplantation.com, US$174–342, depending on cabin size, season, and location, sleeps 2–6, a/c an additional

US$25/day) is three kilometers up and back down a steep dirt road turning north off the highway just west of the entrance to French Harbour. The resort consists of a dozen or so freestanding bungalow houses set amid a shady grove of palms at the edge of a broad, beautiful beach and backed by lush tropical forest. Each of the 19 bungalow houses has 2–3 bedrooms.

The hotel offers dive packages through an on-site branch of the highly regarded dive shop **Subway Watersports** (tel. 504/3387-0579 or 504/445-5707, www.subwaywatersports.com), as well as kayaking and horseback riding to its guests, and has an international restaurant serving three meals a day. All-inclusive packages and weekly rates are available. Provided

## CANOPY TOURS

Short of chartering a private plane for an island tour, taking a canopy ride is one of the best ways to enjoy fantastic views of the island, with an adrenaline rush tossed in for free. Children (as young as four!) are welcome on the canopies – for those that require hand-braking, the child is strapped to a guide. There are several rides on the island from which to choose.

**Gumbalimba** (tel. 504/9914-9196, 8 A.M.-4 P.M. daily, US$45, or US$35 with a ticket to the animal park) has the corner on the West End/West Bay market simply thanks to its location between the two. There are 18 lines that start in the hills and lead down to the beach. The canopy tour takes about an hour, sometimes a bit less, and transportation is included in the price.

Equally convenient, however, is **South Shore Canopy Tour** (tel. 504/9904-7855, southshorecanopy@yahoo.com, 8 A.M.-4 P.M. daily, US$45), a 12-line tour covering three kilometers. The starting point is on the road between West Bay and West End, closest to the West End side. Transportation is included.

Close to Palmetto Bay is the **Jungle Canopy Tour** (tel. 504/445-4151, U.S. tel. 877/540-9692, US$45), with 12 lines, two suspension bridges, and a climbing wall. Speed here is controlled by design rather than your hand-brake, which makes it a bit easier. Children should be at least four feet tall. There is an animal park next door (not as fancy as Gumbalimba, but only a couple of dollars entrance fee).

Surely the most unique of the lot, but rather far-flung for those staying in West End or West Bay, is **Pirates of the Caribbean Canopy** (tel. 504/455-7576, www.roatancanopy-pirates-of-the-caribbean.com, 8 A.M.-5 P.M.

Thrillseekers can explore the treetops of Roatán.

Mon.-Fri.). There are two different rides: The easier version has nine lines, five bridges, and a rock wall (US$45), while the "extreme" has eight long lines totaling 2,683 meters, including one 1,837-meter line, reputed to be the longest in the Americas (US$65). Speed here is controlled by design rather than with hand-brakes. Night tours are available by appointment. There is a free short trial zipline at the entrance for those who want to test the experience before putting their money down. The canopy is east of French Harbour; there are signs right on the highway.

they can get there, the public is welcome to enjoy the beach at Palmetto Bay, as long as they have at least one meal at the restaurant.

The **Jungle Canopy Tour** (tel. 504/445-4151) is nearby.

## East of French Harbour

The narrow, two-lane highway (bicyclists beware) running east of French Harbour to Oak Ridge winds for most of its length along the ridge in the center of the island, affording superb views of both coasts and the reef, visible under the clear water. Between French Harbour and the Punta Gorda turnoff, the highway passes Juticalpa, a small Latino community and the only sizable inland settlement anywhere on the Bay Islands. Once heavily forested, these central island mountain slopes have been almost entirely denuded of their original cover and now support secondary scrub growth, pasture, or farmland.

About a kilometer east of French Harbour, keep an eye out on the right-hand side for a long white fence, at the end of which is a road turning in, with a sign to the **Arch's Iguana Farm** (tel. 504/455-7482, 8 A.M.–5 P.M. daily, US$5), located just over a kilometer (0.8 mile) from the main highway down a paved road. When you come to a fork, make a left onto the dirt road and follow the signs to the end. Here you can check out some amazingly huge (some more than one meter long) iguanas, frequently unnervingly interested in their human visitors, especially if you have banana leaves to share. There is also a large, enclosed deck area for viewing fish (including barracudas and tarpons), turtles (including hawksbill, green back, and loggerhead), and lobsters (which are in a separate section so they can lay eggs and re-populate the surrounding area, decimated by overfishing).

A bit farther east on the highway is the entrance to **The Coco View Resort** (tel. 504/9911-7371, U.S. tel. 800/510-8164, www.cocoviewresort.com, US$1,100–1,390 for weeklong dive packages) which is, along with Anthony's Key Resort, one of the oldest and most popular dive resorts in the Bay Islands.

© AMY E. ROBERTSON

At Arch's Iguana Farm, feeding the iguanas is a popular activity for kids and adults alike.

The hotel offers several room options, including homey, wooden ocean bungalows and larger apartments, built right over the water with lovely porches facing the water and sunset, and another 10 rooms in an oceanfront building, all with air-conditioning. Those looking for a few more amenities can consider renting one of the eight privately owned beach houses nearby, not used by their owners most of the year (U.S. tel. 800/282-8932, www.playmiguel.com). Rates are US$326–627 per person for a week's stay, depending on the property reserved and the number of guests (up to six can be accommodated). Diving is excellent right offshore—the reef wall starts 30 meters from the hotel and the wreck of the 42-meter *Prince Albert* is entombed in 20 meters of water nearby. Close by is the famed diving site *Mary's Place,* usually the culmination of the weeklong schedule of dives. The dive crew is professional and friendly, and Coco View has a fleet of large, well-equipped dive boats, even with a hatch to come up from underneath directly into the boat in rough weather. *Note:* Children under the age of 10 are not allowed at Coco View.

A few kilometers farther east is Milton Bight, home to the dive shop **Subway Watersports** (tel. 504/3387-0579 or 504/413-2229, ask for dive shop, www.subwaywatersports .com), which takes walk-in clients on dives to the many great reef locations near there for US$35 per dive, and trips to the revered site *Mary's Place* are made daily. Kayaking, Jet-Skiing, water-skiing, water-boarding, shark dives, day trips to farther-flung sites (such as Morat, Barbaretta, Utila, the Sea Mounts, and Cayos Cochinos), and fishing trips can all be arranged as well. Subway is a PADI five-star Instructor Development Center, and the first National Geographic dive center in Roatán (the National Geographic courses teach the same diving, with a heavier emphasis on environmental awareness and marine science).

Subway also can arrange accommodation in a number of nearby **vacation homes,** listed on their website, ranging from nice to luxury, and priced accordingly (US$700–5,000/night, some with nightly rates also available). Subway is adjacent to the resort **Turquoise Bay** (tel. 504/413-2229, U.S. tel. 786/623-6121, www .turquoisebayresort.com), whose 26 modern, attractive rooms sprinkled along the hill all offer views of the spectacular bay below. The staff is rather uninspired, and the resort hosts day visits by cruise-shippers, but the breathtaking setting and top-notch dive center make up for the shortcomings. There is a pool and restaurant on-site, and in addition to the water-sport center activities, guests can snorkel, play beach volleyball, or arrange for a horseback ride on the beach. Three-night stays are the minimum, and a week-long package runs US$1,194 per person for divers, US$749 per person for non-divers, both based on double occupancy and costing a bit more during high season.

While plenty of places on the island have water views, the best spot for a view of the island itself is the appropriately named **The View** restaurant, right on the highway not far from the turnoff to the Parrot Tree Plantation. From the peak of a steep hill, the view is of lush emerald vegetation leading down to the golden sand and turquoise water. Vendors sell handicrafts and souvenirs in the small grassy area in front of the restaurant.

While there are plenty of ziplines that for most visitors will be closer to their hotel, parents with pirate-crazy kids might want to check out the **Pirates of the Caribbean Canopy Tour** (tel. 504/455-7576, www.roatan canopy-pirates-of-the-caribbean.com), where buccaneers as young as four can try out the ziplines.

Continuing east toward Jonesville, keep your eyes peeled for a spa sign along the highway that leads to **Spa Tranquilidad** (tel. 504/9797-0042 or 504/3260-7173, www.fuegodelmar .com/spa, by appointment only), a bit out of the way, but with some of the best-value spa services on the island. Professional masseuse Blanca Bodden offers hour-long massages for just US$30, and other treatments like facials, wraps, and stone therapy are available as well. The spa is at Politilly Bight—if you pass the Garífuna center Yubu heading east, then you've gone too far.

A bit out of the way, but worth the trip for an unusual dining experience, is **⟨C Hole in the Wall Restaurant** (tel. 504/3270-3577, www.roatanholeinthewall.com, open for lunch and dinner daily) in Jonesville. To get there, either drive or take a taxi to Jonesville, and get one of the boaters on the dock to take you across to the restaurant, built on a dock right over the water on the far side of the lagoon. The seafood is top-notch, and it's a great place to while away a few hours sipping drinks and chatting with whoever happens to be around the popular restaurant (burgers and sandwiches US$3.70–9, entrées US$9–15). On Sundays at 2:30 P.M. (and usually Fridays too, but call first to confirm), the restaurant offers an all-you-can-eat-until-it's-gone dinner with lobster and/or shrimp, barbecued filet mignon, cole slaw, mashed potatoes, beans, bread, and dessert for US$25. Mangrove tours can be arranged too; Clyde is a local old-timer who gladly takes visitors around and regales them with stories, charging US$7.50 per person for a 40-minute tour. If you're coming in a rented car, take the gravel road from the highway down to Jonesville, then the paved road in Jonesville until you reach a fork in the road—take the left branch. The road ends about 100 meters ahead, where there is a large empty area with some houses bordering the sea. Park your car here, and if it's still light out, knock on the turquoise house on the left, whose residents will radio the restaurant to pick you up. After sundown, you'll need to call the restaurant for a pickup (if you don't have a cell phone, ask your hotel to make this call before you hit the road).

## PUNTA GORDA

The oldest permanent settlement in Roatán, Punta Gorda ("Fat Point") was founded shortly after April 12, 1797, when some 3,000 Garífuna deportees from the Caribbean island of San Vicente were stranded on Roatán by the British. After settling in Punta Gorda, many Garífuna continued on, migrating to Trujillo and from there up and down the Caribbean coasts of Honduras, Nicaragua, Guatemala, and Belize, but their first Honduran home remained. The anniversary marking their arrival is cause for great celebration in Punta Gorda. Garífuna from all over the coast attend the event. For most of the year, though, Punta Gorda is simply a sleepy seaside town—dozens of *cayucos* pulled up on the beach, a steady breeze blowing in the palms, and Garífuna residents moving at a very deliberate pace, usually happy to spend a few minutes or hours chatting with a visitor. The only visible evidence of the town's history is a modest statue of Satuyé, the revered Garífuna warrior on San Vicente, located at the entrance to town from the highway.

The beaches in town are not very clean, but not far up the coast you'll find fine patches of open sand, like Camp Bay Beach to the east. Local boat owners will take you there for a negotiable fee. There's snorkeling and diving on the reef near Punta Gorda, but it's for strong swimmers only. Watch out for boat traffic if you swim across the bay to the reef, and remember that the north side of Roatán is choppier than the south and west.

### Practicalities

On the main road looping through town (both ends connect to the highway) are a few *pulperías* and *comedores*, a pool hall, and a couple of hotels. It's hard to imagine a reason why anyone would stay here over another place with better beaches and services, but if fate brings you here, the best rooms in town are at **North Side Garden** (tel. 504/435-1848, US$16 s/d, cold water only), in a reasonably attractive two-story wooden house with five tidy rooms, each with a TV, fan and one double bed.

Toward the eastern end of town is **Dayia Internet Café** (8 A.M.–9 P.M. Mon.–Sat., sometimes open Sundays), charging US$2 an hour for Internet.

Although not as frequently patronized as the Oak Ridge boaters, locals will gladly arrange a **boat tour** of the mangrove tunnels and waterways—teeming with wildlife—costing maybe US$15–20 for an hour's trip, depending on negotiating skills and fuel prices.

Back up at the highway is Satuye Park, which, on days that cruise ships are in, has a handful of **handicraft and souvenir** vendors.

# OAK RIDGE

From the highway coming downhill to the water's edge, it seems Oak Ridge is scattered all over the place, clinging to hillsides, cays, and peninsulas all around a large harbor, which is literally the center of town. The harbor has always been the town's entire reason for existence, first serving as a refuge for pirates fleeing Spanish warships, then as the center of a major boat-building industry, and now as home to a fishing fleet and processing plant. Oak Ridge is the capital of the José Santos Guardiola municipality, which covers eastern Roatán.

Perhaps because of its relative remoteness (it's about a 40-minute drive from Coxen Hole to Oak Ridge), more of Oak Ridge's 5,000 residents are obviously of English descent than elsewhere in Roatán. But Spanish-speaking immigrants are beginning to settle in Oak Ridge, particularly along the highway coming into town. Though not a major tourist destination, Oak Ridge is near plenty of pristine, little-known dive sites on the southern and eastern Roatán reef. Two local dive resorts welcome walk-in divers. There are extensive mangrove swamps near town, which can be visited by hiring local boats.

## Practicalities

Buses stop at the mainland dock next to a **BGA** (which changes cash and travelers checks and advances money on Visa cards) and the fish-processing plant. From there, a visitor can walk along the shore, past the fish plant all the way around the western end of the harbor, over a small bridge, and out to a narrow point facing the ocean.

Apart from a couple of stores and a weather-beaten wooden church, there's not much on the point, though it's interesting to check out the town and docks. The ocean-facing side of the point has no beach, only exposed, rocky coral, which makes it difficult to get out to snorkel on the reef.

At last check, no budget hotels were open in Oak Ridge, though you might find a room by asking around. For food, however, **BJ's Backyard** (www.roatanonline.com/bj-backyard), on the waterfront, is a local institution. B. J. herself is quite a character, and she turns out great fish sandwiches, served on homemade bread. To get there, take the road from the highway toward Oak Ridge, bear right, then look for the sign on the left. If you reach the Hondutel office, you've gone too far. Mangrove tours can be arranged at BJ's as well.

From the dock by the bus stop, **water taxis** will take a visitor over to the cay ("cayside") for US$1 or so, though some drivers may try to charge you more. Cayside is much the same as the point; several houses sit among the trees behind the rocky, coral-covered shoreline.

Most cayside tourist visitors are coming to the ( **Reef House Resort** (tel. 504/435-1482, U.S. tel. 866/478-4888, www.reefhouseresort.com, weeklong dive and meal packages for US$1,038 pp for a couple), one of the oldest dive resorts on the island—but a well-maintained one, having seen recent renovations. Technically, it's not on Roatán, but on Oakridge Cay, a tiny island a five-minute boat-ride away. The owners dive many little-known south-side sites nearby, including an excellent wall right in front of the hotel. The dive packages include three boat dives daily and unlimited shore diving. Daily rates (which still include all meals) are US$157 nondiver and US$168 diver; and packages can be arranged for any length of stay. Come prepared with your own entertainment (a couple of good books? a deck of cards? a watercolor set to paint the landscape?) for when you're not diving or snorkeling.

## Near Oak Ridge

Not far from town in both directions, but especially east, are several beaches. Dory captains on the main dock near the bus stop will transport you there for US$10 return. Longer trips to Barbareta, Pigeon Cay (off Barbareta), Helene, Port Royal, or through the mangrove canals are also possible, for negotiable fees. The mangrove tunnels, formerly used by pirates to hide from their pursuers and now filled with all sorts of wildlife, are frequently recommended as a great trip, usually costing around US$15 an hour. Make sure you agree on the amount of time beforehand, as there have been reports of boatmen giving only 15-minute tours.

# EASTERN ROATÁN

## Paya Bay

Between Oak Ridge and Punta Gorda, a dirt road turns off the highway to the east, marked by a sign for the **Paya Bay Beach and Dive Resort** (tel. 504/435-1037, U.S. tel. 866/323-5414, www.payabay.com, US$1,479 pp for weeklong dive packages, US$1,247 for nondivers). Far, far off the beaten path, this small hotel is set on a bluff above the ocean, at the point of two lovely, secluded beach-fronted bays. While the decor is a bit dated, who's looking at the furniture when every room has a water view and balcony? The steady breezes keep the rooms cool day and night, although all rooms also have air-conditioning. Daily rates are available, and the nightly rate for room-only is US$150, with dives US$35 each. The dive shop has gear for 30 people and offers Open Water certification; guests can dive many infrequently visited sites on the north side and around Barbareta. Flatsfishing and hiking are available as well as the usual snorkel and scuba. The resort claims to be at its most stunning leading up to and during the full moon and, conveniently, lists those dates on its website, as well as the dates of its "naturist" (clothing-optional) weeks.

## Port Royal

The dirt road continues past Camp Bay over the hills to Port Royal, once the site of English pirate camps, now the site of luxury homes for wealthy Hondurans and retired expatriates. Named for the famous port in Jamaica, Port Royal was long the favorite anchorage for marauding pirates because of its protected, defensible harbor. It was chosen by the British military as its base in the 1740s for the same reasons. The British built two small forts to guard the harbor: Fort Frederick on the mainland, with one rampart and six cannons, and Fort George on the cay, with one rampart and 17 cannons. In spite of their heavy armaments, the forts didn't see much service before their destruction in 1782 by a Spanish expedition. The remains of Fort George can still be seen, while the foundations for Fort Frederick now hold a private home.

Currently, no lodgings or restaurants exist in Port Royal, but the mega-resort **Princesa de Roatan** is under construction.

**Old Port Royal,** farther east, is thought to be the site of the ill-fated Providence Company settlement, dating from the 1630s and 1640s. This is the deepest harbor on the island, though it's no longer used for commerce.

The hills above Port Royal were declared the **Port Royal Park and Wildlife Refuge** in 1978 in an effort to protect the principal watershed for eastern Roatán and several species of endangered wildlife. The refuge has no developed trails for hikers.

## East End Islands

East of Port Royal, Roatán peters out into a lowland mangrove swamp, impassable by foot or car, which connects to the island of **Helene,** sometimes called Santa Helena. Just east of Helene is the smaller island of **Morat,** and farther east is **Barbareta,** a two- by five-kilometer island, home to pristine virgin island forest and several lovely beaches. All three islands are surrounded by spectacular reef. A resort once operated on Barbareta, but in recent years the island has become known as a way station for drug runners, and the resort owner wisely decamped.

Southeast of Barbareta are the **Pigeon Cays,** a perfect spot for a relaxed day of picnicking and snorkeling with no one around. Boats to Barbareta, Morat, Helene, and the Pigeon Cays can be hired at the main dock in Oak Ridge.

# Utila

Utila feels lost in a tropical time warp. Listening to the broad, almost incomprehensible Caribbean English coming out of islanders with names like Morgan and Bodden, it seems pirates ran amok here just a few years back instead of three centuries ago. Life on Utila still moves at a sedate pace; local conversation is dominated by the weather, the state of the fishing industry, and spicy gossip about the affairs of the 2,000 or so inhabitants.

In the past couple of decades, Utila has gradually come face to face with the modern day. A steadily growing stream of budget travelers flow in from across the globe, all eager to get scuba certification for as little money as possible (about US$270 in early 209, including dorm-style accommodation) and to enjoy the balmy Caribbean waters and famed reef. With its semiofficial designation as the low-budget Bay Island, Utila has become one of those backpacker hot spots like Zipolite or Lake Atitlán—packed with young Europeans and Americans out for a good time in the sun.

Utila is also well known among sea life enthusiasts as one of the best places in the world to see the **whale shark,** the largest fish in the world. These monstrous creatures, getting as big as 15 meters, frequent the Cayman Channel right off Utila and can be spotted (with much patience and a good captain) frequently throughout the year, and particularly in April, May, August, and September.

Timing can be hugely important in making sure that you have the vacation you were looking for in Utila. The rainy season stretches from mid-September to mid-December. Visibility is lower when diving during this season, but reasonable, while snorkeling can be flat-out unappetizing due to the colder weather. The hottest months tend to be April and May. If you do visit during the rainy season, bring a pair of Crocs or other rubber clogs; regular shoes will get muddy and wet, while flip-flops fling droplets of sandy mud up the backs of your calves while you walk.

The opportunity to snorkel with whale

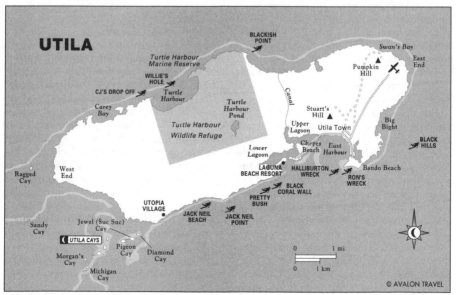

sharks is one of those once-in-a-lifetime travel experiences and, for many, the reason they choose Utila over any other Caribbean island—whale sharks are frequent visitors on the island's north coast. That said, no matter what any hotel or dive shop claims, there is never a guarantee about spotting one, even during the April–May whale shark high season.

Many businesses cater to low-budget travelers, and many of those offer excellent values for their services, be it a dive course, US$10 hotel room, or luscious fish dinner. More recently, slightly more upscale visitors have started arriving, and local hotels and restaurants are beginning to increase their services to this market as a result. But the international backpacker party scene is as strong as ever and will undoubtedly continue for years to come. The majority of backpackers are European, although there are large American and Canadian contingencies as well.

The smallest of the three main Bay Islands, Utila is 11 kilometers long and 5 kilometers wide, with two-thirds of its area covered by swamp. Two small hills on the eastern part of the island, Pumpkin Hill and Stuart's Hill, are volcanic in origin. Sand flies can be voracious on Utila, so come prepared (some swear by Avon's Skin So Soft mixed with a light—10 percent or less—DEET repellent). Just remember that the DEET damages coral; rinse off before you head into the water.

As in Roatán, the Utila reef is under threat from fishermen and careless divers, to say nothing of water pollution. But without the steep hillsides of Roatán and still plenty of undrained wetlands, Utila is not likely to face as serious a water quality problem, at least in the near future. The Bay Islands Conservation Association (BICA) in Utila patrols the entire reef around the island, with the exception of the shallow waters around the cays, where only local residents are allowed to fish. BICA also pays for environmental education in schools and sets up mooring buoys for diver boats.

Utila's name reputedly derives from a contraction of *ocotillo*, which in Nahuatl refers to a place with a lot of black smoke. The smoke is thought to have come from burning the resinous *ocote* pine, supposedly used by pre-Columbian islanders in a type of distilling process.

A good general source of information about Utila can be found at www.aboututila.com, which includes descriptions of dive sites and current average dive prices, as well as information about hotels, restaurants, and other businesses. The website www.utilaeastwind.com is the online home of Utila's monthly local newspaper, and is a good source of info on the island (from local news to restaurant reviews, movie showings, hotel prices, and a directory of phone numbers). The BICA website, www.bicautila.org, also has information on the environment of the island and the reef.

Utila hosts its annual **Carnival** the last full week of July. There are cultural and sporting events, a community bonfire at Chepes beach, and various street parties held in local neighborhoods. Restaurants stay open later, and a few bars even stay open 24 hours a day. If you have a particular accommodation in mind, it's best to reserve well in advance, but the smallest hotels do not typically take reservations, and there's always a room to be found.

## UTILA TOWN (EAST HARBOUR)

Almost all Utilians live in East Harbour, on the south side of the island. Universally known simply as Utila, the town wraps around a large harbor that's protected from the open ocean by an arm of reef. The town is divided into four parts: the Point, between the old airport and downtown; Sandy Bay, between the center and the Chepes Beach; the Center, near the main intersection and the municipal dock; and Cola de Mico (meaning Monkey Tail) Road, which cuts inland perpendicular to the shore and leads to the current airstrip. Connecting the old airport, downtown, and Sandy Bay is Main Street. Mamey Lane Road, leaving Main Street in Sandy Bay, also heads inland to the north, roughly parallel to Cola de Mico Road.

Although not a large town in total population, Utila's collection of wooden houses, dive shops, hotels, and restaurants is spread across

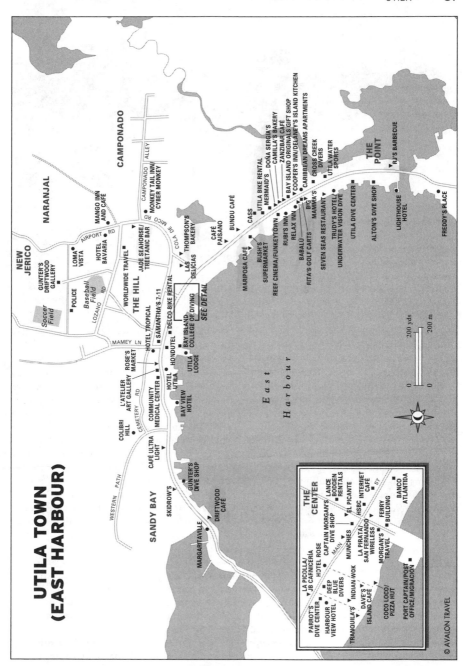

UTILA TOWN
(EAST HARBOUR)

NARANJAL

NEW JERICO

CAMPONADO

THE POINT

RJ'S BARBECUE

UTILA WATER SPORTS
CROSS CREEK DIVERS
CARIBBEAN DREAMS APARTMENTS
COOPER'S INN/DELANEY'S ISLAND KITCHEN
BAY ISLAND ORIGINALS GIFT SHOP
ZANZIBAR CAFÉ
CAMILLA'S BAKERY
DONA SERGIA'S
MERMAID'S
UTILA BIKE RENTAL
REEF CINEMA/FUNKEYTOWN
BUSH'S SUPERMARKET

MANGO INN AND CAFÉ

MONKEY TAIL INN/CYBER MONKEY
CAMPONADO ALLEY

CALLE DE MICO RD

JADE SEAHORSE/TRETANIC BAR

LOMA VISTA
HOTEL BAVARIA

AIRPORT RD

GUNTER'S DRIFTWOOD GALLERY

POLICE

Baseball Field

Soccer Field

LOZANO RD

THE HILL

WORLDWIDE TRAVEL

BUNDU CAFÉ

CAFÉ PAISANO

LAS DELICIAS

THOMPSON'S BAKERY

CASS

MARIPOSA CAFÉ

RUBI'S INN

RELAX INN

BABALU

BIG MAMMA'S

TRUDY'S HOTEL/UNDERWATER VISION DIVE

SEVEN SEAS RESTAURANT

RITA'S GOLF CARTS

UTILA DIVE CENTER

ALTON'S DIVE SHOP

LIGHTHOUSE HOTEL

FREDDY'S PLACE

SAMANTHA'S 7-11

HOTEL TROPICAL

DELCO BIKE RENTAL

HONDUTEL

UTILA LODGE

BAY ISLAND COLLEGE OF DIVING

SEE DETAIL

MAMEY LN

ROSE'S MARKET

HOTEL UTILA

BAY VIEW HOTEL

L'ATELIER ART GALLERY

COLIBRI HILL

CEMETERY RD

COMMUNITY MEDICAL CENTER

CAFÉ ULTRA LIGHT

SANDY BAY

WESTERN PATH

SKIDROW'S

GUNTER'S DIVE SHOP

DRIFTWOOD CAFÉ

MARGARTAVILLE

E a s t   H a r b o u r

200 yds

200 m

THE CENTER

PARROT'S DIVE CENTER

HARBOUR VIEW HOTEL

DEEP BLUE DIVERS

TRANQUILA'S

INDIAN WOK

DAVE'S ISLAND CAFÉ

COCO LOCO/PIZZA HUT

LA PICOLLA/JB CARNICERIA

HOTEL ROSE

CAPTAIN MORGAN'S DIVE SHOP

MAIN

MUNCHIES

EL PICANTE

LA PIRATA/SAN FERNANDO

MORGAN'S TRAVEL

HSBC

WIRELESS

LANCE BODDEN RENTALS

INTERNET CAFÉ

S7

FERRY BUILDING

BANCO ATLANTIDA

PORT CAPTAIN/POST OFFICE/MIGRACIÓN

© AVALON TRAVEL

the town of East Harbour, universally known simply as Utila

a largish area. While it's easy enough to walk, renting a bike, golf cart, or scooter can be a fun way to cover the ground between your hotel, dive shop, and favorite restaurants and bars.

While the booming dive industry has brought a lot of money to Utila, native Utilians continue to struggle, especially as all-inclusive dive shops crowd out family-owned hotels and restaurants. Travelers can be sensitive to this situation by making sure to frequent some locally owned businesses during their visit.

Visitors may notice that, unlike everywhere else in Honduras, baseball, not soccer, is the sport of choice on Utila. If you want one of those bonding sports conversations, a pertinent comment on the major leagues will help kick things off.

## RECREATION
### Dive Shops
If there's any complaint to be leveled against Utila, it's that all anyone ever talks about is diving. All things considered, that's no surprise. Word has gotten out that Utila offers one of the least expensive Open Water scuba

certifications in the world, and business has been booming ever since. Competition between shops is fierce, with employees sometimes pursuing potential clients at the docks and on the streets. A whopping 14 shops were in business in Utila at last count. All the competition is wonderful news to the discerning would-be diver, who would be wise to ignore the touts that meet the ferries at the dock and instead spend a bit of time wandering through town, asking around among other travelers and checking out several dive shops before deciding where to go and what courses to take.

*Note:* Although they are extremely rare, especially considering the very high number of divers passing through the Bay Islands, accidents—including fatal accidents—have occurred on both islands. One advantage of making sure your dive shop is certified by PADI, SSI, or NAUI is that all accidents must be reported and investigated, while noncertified shops can simply fire the dive master/instructor and hire another.

It is certainly true that some shops are more diligent than others, particularly regarding

# DIVING UTILA'S REEF

Utila's south-side fringing reef starts relatively close to shore, with tongue-and-groove formations of hard corals in a few meters of water sloping down to the bottom of the reef wall at around 20 meters. Farther south from Utila are numerous sea mounts ringed with reef, known for some of the finest soft corals found in the Bay Islands. Similar to Roatán and Guanaja, Utila's north-side reef is separated from the shore by a lagoon of varying size. The sandy bottom gradually begins to fill in with coral until the reef wall is reached, almost breaking the water surface in places. On the north side, with particularly good dive sites around Turtle Harbour, the wall plunges hundreds of meters over the edge of the continental shelf. Giant sponges and pillar coral are common. Off the east side of Utila are long ridges of elkhorn coral.

Most of Utila's divers frequent sites on the south side of the island, simply because they are quicker and easier to get to from East Harbour than the north side, and also the waters are more protected and tend to be calmer. Ask around for dive shops going to north-side sites, as well as to sea mounts south of the island. Captain Morgan's Dive Shop on Jewel Cay tends to get to the north side more often, by virtue of its location.

## SOUTH SIDE

**Jack Neil Point** and **Jack Neil Beach** are both great long, shallow dives along the tongue-and-groove formations of hard and soft corals. At the western end of the reef here, sightings of hawksbill and green turtles are common.

Among the many similar dives along the southern wall, each starting in around 4 meters of water and dropping to about 30 meters at the base of the reef, **Pretty Bush** and **Black Coral Wall** are two good ones. Despite the name of the latter dive, young black coral is found all along the wall here, as are elkhorn and pillar coral, sea fans, and frequent spot-ted eagle rays cruising at the deeper sections along the reef wall.

## NEAR THE OLD AIRPORT

Right off the point by the old Airport, **Ron's Wreck** isn't all that impressive as wrecks go, but the real attraction is the thriving sea life in the vicinity. A few hundred meters west is another, larger wreck, the **Halliburton,** sunk in 1998 by the local dive association, where careful divers can explore the pilot house and some of the decks.

Farther offshore from the airport, in fact not always easily found by the dive-boat captains, is one of Utila's most popular sites, **Black Hills,** a luscious and varied patch of coral crowning a sea mount. Sharks are common, attracted by the schools of fish that frequent the sea mount.

## NORTH SIDE

**CJ's Drop Off,** at the western end of the reef in front of Turtle Harbour, is famed among divers for the vertigo-inducing coral cliffs plunging straight down into the blue depths. As you descend along the wall, watch for sting rays, moray eels, and hawksbill turtles, and the profusion of giant sponges and hard corals. Be sure to also keep a close eye on that depth gauge as it's easy to lose track with no bottom in sight.

Another popular dive a bit farther east along the same stretch of reef is **Willie's Hole,** a dramatic open cave in the coral wall at around 25 meters, with plenty of pillar and star corals to admire, along with sponges. Don't be surprised to see schools of snapper, jack, and spade fish cruising right past you.

Near the entrance to the old cross-island canal, at the western end of Rock Harbour, is **Blackish Point,** a system of caverns and passages in the reef wall at around 20 meters, with encrusted overhangs to check out. The gentle current makes this a good drift dive.

quality of instructors and upkeep of equipment. Don't make your decision based on price, or at least not exclusively, as most courses and dives cost about the same in the good shops—instead, focus on the background of the instructors (most important), the quality of equipment and boat, your rapport with the dive shop staff, and the quality of the accommodations.

Those who worry about decompression sickness will be glad to hear that Utila has its own **hyperbaric chamber** at the Bay Islands College of Diving (tel. 504/425-3378, VHF channel 71).

Most shops are PADI-certified, and a few have other certifications (SSI and NAUI) as well. Prices currently stand at US$270 for an Open Water or Advanced Open Water course, including accommodations. Those whose prices are slightly higher typically include more things—such as the required PADI notebook (US$7), the daily reef tax (US$4), and drinking water—or have better accommodations. Most classrooms have air-conditioning, which is key if you are on Utila in April or May. If you're penny-pinching and plan to take advantage of the free accommodation offers, note that a few shops charge US$3 for the first night's stay, some of the dorms are cleaner and more pleasant than others, and a few have hot water. If you are looking for a little more comfort (and a bathroom in your room), consider springing for a private hotel room, either at your shop's affiliated hotel (many shops can get their students a discount) or at a hotel elsewhere in town.

Fun dives currently run US$55 for two (plus the reef tax), and 10-dive packages run US$220–250. Most shops have Open Water courses starting every day, available in English, Spanish, French, Italian, Dutch, and a surprising number of other languages as well—take time to check it out if you are looking for a particular language. (Japanese? Check. Swiss German? Check.)

All of the shops here are PADI-certified and have close to the same prices for all services.

**Alton's Dive Center** (tel. 504/425-3704, www.diveinutila.com) was named by its former

Sea turtles are easily spotted in the waters around the Bay Islands.

© JOZEF MAERIEN

owner but is now run by a friendly German-Canadian couple who are especially committed to sound environmental practices. PADI certifications are of course available (US$249, including manuals and accommodations but not reef tax), but most notably, Alton's is the only shop on the island offering certifications with NAUI, an organization considered by many to have the highest standards for diving safety (see www.naui.org for more information). Instructors typically have dive counts in the thousands, and readers have reported very positive experiences with the staff. There are kayaks and snorkel equipment available, but for an extra charge. The dorms are not the best in town, nor the cleanest, but acceptable.

Dive masters at **Bay Islands College of Diving** (tel. 504/425-3291, www.dive-utila .com) are pros, and classes are kept small. At the time of our visit, the equipment was very new, and in 2005 the shop won an award for its environmental practices. Like Utila Dive Centre, the college can certify divers all the way up to instructor level. The confined-water

dives are done in the shop's indoor pool—a plus for those studying to be instructors, but perhaps less appealing for those in the Open Water certification courses. There is also a Jacuzzi, ideal for relaxing at the end of a long dive day, especially during the cooler rainy season. The only hyperbaric chamber and trauma center on Utila is located at this dive shop (in case you are unlucky enough to get the bends), although it is open to use for any diver in case of emergency. The free accommodation is in the slightly depressing motel-style Hotel Utila, which has fairly steep rates (US$17 s, US$20 d) for those staying on additional nights—but BICD is building its own dorm. This is also the dive shop that forms part of the very nice, but much pricier, Utila Lodge Dive Resort. Boats are spacious and well-maintained.

**Captain Morgan's Dive Shop** (office near the municipal dock in East Harbour, tel. 504/425-3349, www.divingutila.com) is a bit farther afield than most, run out of the Hotel Kayla on Jewel Cay, a small, tranquil island (with a bit fewer sand fleas) a half-hour boat

© PETER SVANBERG

A dive boat awaits its morning passengers.

ride from East Harbour. All rooms at the hotel have a private bath with cold water, and there is a shared fridge, microwave, and toaster oven. The shop, which has two dive boats, is a great

place for those who prefer a quieter scene, and trips into town are easily arranged. Its location makes it a lot easier to reach some of the north coast dive sites, considered by many to be the island's best.

**Cross Creek** (tel. 504/425-3397, www.cross creekutila.com) has the same owner as the Utila Dive Center, but a different vibe, with an entire complex built over the lagoon stretching out behind the shop office. Equipment looks well-maintained, as do the boats, the largest of which is 39 feet and can accommodate 20 divers. They have prescription masks for contact lens wearers. Accommodations are on-site, the free dorm rooms in a long cabin with hammocks hanging in the breezeway. Rooms are acceptable, although not spotless, and a few have their own bathroom (although both the shared and private bath are cold-water only). There's a separate dive master cabin with hot water and—a big step up—four "deluxe" rooms (US$30), in separate cabins built on decks over the mangroves and lagoon, with TVs, hot water, air-conditioning, and minifridges.

**Deep Blue Divers** (tel. 504/425-3211, www.DeepBlueUtila.com) is a five-star Gold Palm IDC Center, meaning that certification all the way through dive instructor is offered here. The office location is near-perfect for the party crowd: wedged between the island's two most popular bars, Coco Loco and Tranquilo. Class size is limited to just four (although an exception can be made if a group of five friends wants to have the class together). The beginning Open Water certification course is US$249. The shop offers accommodations at a variety of hotels, some with an additional charge (for better rooms).

**Ecomarine Gunter's Dive Shop** (in Sandy Bay, tel. 504/425-3350, ecomar@gmail.com) offers the beginner's Open Water course for US$259 including two free fun dives as well as accommodation (but not including the reef tax). Kayaks and snorkel equipment are available for rent, and nondivers can ride out on dive boats for a snorkel trip for US$10 (plus equipment rental). Students are put up in the

## DIVING RULES AND ETIQUETTE

- Don't dive alone.

- Know your limitations, and only dive if you're in good physical condition.

- Always follow the dive tables.

- Don't anchor anywhere in or near coral – use the buoys.

- Don't litter or discharge foreign substances into the water.

- When diving, always fly a diver-down flag and lower the flag when all divers are back on board. When passing moored boats, or boats flying a diving flag, always pass on the seaward side at least 50 meters (150 feet) away, even in a small boat.

- Avoid contact with any living part of the reef.

- Always observe proper buoyancy techniques and secure dangling equipment.

- Never sit or stand on coral formations, or grab coral to steady yourself.

- Don't grab, poke, ride, or chase reef inhabitants.

- Don't feed the fish.

- Don't fish on the reef.

- Don't remove any marine organisms, alive or dead.

- If you find garbage on the reef, gently remove it and bring it back to shore.

- Take only photographs; leave only bubbles.

Backpacker Lodge across the street, which is clean and decent, although cold-water only. Dorm rooms here are US$4 for nondivers, while private rooms are US$10 for nondivers. **Parrots Dive Centre** (tel. 504/425-3772, TatianaLuna22@yahoo.com) is a locally owned dive shop, with a few of those rarest of breeds—Utilian dive instructors. Their accommodations are all private rooms, although always with a shared bath. They have laundry service, as well as a shared kitchen (with two stoves, but never enough forks). Additional nights beyond a course are just US$2, and nondivers can stay for the same rock-bottom price (a room doesn't get any cheaper than this!). There is a doctor on the premises 24/7, and the instructors are highly experienced, most of them having worked at the center for years, in contrast with the high turnover of staff at many other shops. Prices are a touch cheaper than at other centers: US$259 for Open Water certification, night dives for US$40, and 10-dive packages for US$220. Kayaks and snorkeling are free. Parrots is also appealingly located on the same pier as Tranquila's Bar and the Indian Wok.

**Underwater Vision** (tel. 504/425-3103, www.underwatervision.net) is also locally owned, set on the East Harbour beach front, around a large patch of sand (volleyball net included). The one-day Discover Scuba Diving class is US$80, and the beginner's Open Water course is US$248. The boats are a bit older than at other shops. Free accommodations are at the adjacent Trudy's Hotel, which offers hot showers to guests in the dorms; priceless at the end of a diving day during the rainy season. Private rooms are also available, US$25 for dive students, US$35 otherwise, with funky fish murals, ceiling fans, polished wood floors, and hot water. The breezeway shelters Adirondack chairs and hammocks perfect for relaxing at the end of a challenging day. There are also private rooms with rather grimy, cold-water showers, which can be had as part of the free accommodation in lieu of the dorm.

**Utila Dive Centre** (on the Point, tel. 504/425-3326, www.utiladivecentre.com)

was the first dive shop opened on the island, in 1991, and is a highly respected shop. In addition to the standard offerings, the shop offers Trimix (a nitrogen-oxygen mix that allows divers to go deeper) and is one of two shops to certify instructors (Bay Islands College of Diving also offers instructor certification). Frequent north-side trips on two 12-meter cabin cruisers are offered; dorm accommodation is at the Mango Inn, including a simple fruit and toast breakfast. While the beginner's Open Water certification (US$279) is a 3.5-day course at most shops, UDC likes to provide a more relaxed pace, taking 4.5 days, and four nights' accommodation are included rather than three.

**Utila Water Sports** (on the Point, tel. 504/425-3264, www.utilawatersports.com) is one of the few locally owned dive shops, and it has safety-conscious, friendly instructors and several large, very well-maintained dive boats (which they share with the Laguna Beach Resort, under the same ownership). The PADI course is US$249, with four free fun dives, while the SSI course is US$224 (cheaper because it doesn't require the purchase of any books or manuals). The maximum student-teacher ratio is five to one. New accommodations are nearing completion, although hot water was still just an idea rather than a reality. An extra night in the dorm accommodation is US$6, while private rooms are US$12 (US$25 if you're not taking a dive course). The shop also rents out sea kayaks and offers dive trips to the Cayos Cochinos.

Shops selling dive gear include Utila Water Sports, Cross Creek, Utila Dive Centre, and Bay Islands College of Diving. For more information on dive shops and diving in Utila, check out the website www.aboututila.com.

## Beaches and Snorkeling

If you take the road east from the center of town, you'll eventually get to **Bando Beach** on the southeastern corner of the island, a groomed, golden beach with several shady *champas* dotting the sand and a large bar *champa* at the entrance. They have public showers and bathrooms and rent snorkel equipment (US$5/

day), kayaks (US$3–5/hour), and paddleboats. Entrance to the beach is US$3 per person. This is the place to be on New Year's Eve.

White-sand **Chepes Beach,** past Sandy Bay on the way out toward Blue Bayou, has a couple of thatch-roof, open-air restaurants, as well as **Patrick's Water Sports** (tel. 504/425-3244), renting Jet-Skis (US$63/hour, US$37/half-hour for two-person; US$79/hour, US$47/half-hour for three-person) and water bananas (US$5.25 pp for a 20-minute ride, with five people max).

Visitors can snorkel at Blue Bayou, a 20-minute walk west of town along the shore, near the mouth of the canal, and at Bando Beach, on the southeastern corner of the island. It's also possible to get in the water at Big Bight, a half-hour walk north of the old airport on the east side of the island, along an unpaved dirt road. You won't see as much colorful coral as on the south-side reef, but rather long ridges of rock and coral, with forests of elkhorn and staghorn coral. Snorkeling and swimming at the airport and Big Bight can be tricky, as the dead coral comes right up to the shore.

All the dive shops rent out snorkel gear for around US$5–7 a day, and many offer it for free if you are diving with them and just want to take a break from scuba. Many will also allow snorkelers to come out on appropriate dives to snorkel while the others scuba.

## Kayaking, Boating, and Fishing

Light sea kayaks make a fine way to explore the canals in the center of the island or to tie off at dive buoys and snorkel. Make sure to get detailed directions to find the southern mouth of the cross-island canal, as it can be tricky to locate.

Besides the kayaks at Bando Beach, **Ecomarine Gunter's** (tel. 504/425-3350) and **Cross Creek** (tel. 504/425-3134) both rent sea kayaks for US$7 half-day, US$10 full-day, slightly more for a double kayak.

*Note:* Visitors should take good care when paddling out into the open water on sea kayaks. Choppy waters and ocean winds can quickly get the better of inexperienced kayakers. If in any doubt at all, stick close to shore and be

A tourist shows off her catch, a giant red snapper.

© SARAH STEINBERG

absolutely sure you have enough energy not only to get out, but to get back, too.

Yacht skippers should call VHF channel 16 to request check-in and clearance-procedure information with Utila Harbour Authority (in Spanish), or go visit the port captain's office next to the police station. Anchoring is permitted in East Harbour and in the Utila Cays Channel for a US$10 monthly fee; always use anchor lights, and do not empty bilges in the harbor or near land. Larger boats may dock at the municipal wharf for a daily docking fee, or get in touch with Troy Bodden at the fuel dock (tel. 504/425-3264), who has water and power hookups for free, but only to take on fuel and water and shop in town. The owners of Utila Lodge (tel. 504/425-3143) can also help find a place to dock.

Fishing trips can be arranged through local fishermen, and lots of signs are up around town. Tarpon, bone fish, mullet, white pompano, and flying fish are all common to the waters around Utila. Fishermen are also happy to arrange trips to the Utila Cays.

## Walks and Exploration

The point at Blue Bayou, a 20-minute walk west of town, marks the southern entrance to the cross-island canal, which is fast closing up because it was man-made and now mangrove cutting is illegal. With considerable effort and a local guide, it may still be possible to get up the canal and across a trail to the west to **Turtle Harbour Pond,** in the center of the island. On the north side of the island west of where the canal lets out are a couple of small, deserted beaches accessible by boat only.

From the end of Cola de Mico Road, a paved road continues four kilometers out to the airport, where it is possible to walk across the airstrip to the beach on the north coast and continue west to **Pumpkin Hill Beach.** Much of the coast here is covered with fossilized coral and rocks, but a few patches of sand provide good spots to put down a towel and relax in splendid isolation. Negotiating a safe passage into the water to swim and snorkel is no easy task, but in calm weather the determined will

make it. Near the beach is **Pumpkin Hill,** 82 meters high and riddled with caves, one of which is the sizable **Brandon Hill Cave,** reputedly containing pirate treasure. When the weather is dry, a dirt road continues back toward Utila Town, a shorter return than via the airport, but a complete mud bog when it has been raining.

Closer to town is **Stuart's Hill,** like Pumpkin Hill a former volcano. From the top are good views over town and the south side of the island.

## Horseback Riding

**Red Ridge Horse Stables** (tel. 504/425-3143 or 504/3390-4817, kisty@utilalodge.com) offers two-hour rides that explore the beach and some local caves, for US$25–35. Riders can sign up at any dive shop. Same day rides can often be arranged, if you haven't reserved in advance.

## ENTERTAINMENT
## C Nightlife

With such an eclectic assortment of young travelers from around the globe, as well as a sizable population of fun-loving locals, it's no surprise that Utila has a flourishing nightlife. While the favored location varies depending on one's mood during the week, Friday night invariably sees a large crowd at the **Bar in the Bush,** literally in the bush at the outskirts of town on Cola de Mico Road, a 15-minute walk from the waterfront. The sprawling cabaña complex, with an attached volleyball court, has an unusually loose, festive ambiance, with an odd mix of people wandering about with drinks in hand, enjoying the grooving music. It's open Wednesdays and Fridays only ("9 P.M. till late"). The bar is a few minutes walk on a dark road heading out of town; walking alone back to your hotel is not recommended.

About the favorite bar in town with foreign visitors is **Tranquila Bar** (3 P.M.–midnight Sun.–Thurs., 3 P.M.–3 A.M. Fri.–Sat.), offering one of the few full bars on the island, with a variety of premium liquors, 25 creatively named shooters (Swamp Water, Chameleon, Scooby

## THE BODDENS

Spend any time on Utila, and you'll soon notice that Bodden is a well-distributed last name. Boddens on Roatán as well. And wait, again in the Mosquitia.

The original Boddens came from the Cayman Islands – the first as a deserter of Oliver Cromwell's army, when it took Jamaica in 1655. His grandson Isaac Bodden was born on Grand Cayman around 1700, and was the first recorded permanent inhabitant of the Cayman Islands.

Settlers came from the Caymans to Utila and Roatán around 1835, bringing their Bodden surname with them (the surname Cooper arrived at the same time, thanks to the immigration of Joseph Cooper, his wife, and their nine children, Brits who arrived to Utila via the Cayman Islands).

Far away on the Mosquitia, in the tiny community of Raistá, there are Miskitos that also bear the last name Bodden. Nearly a century ago, a young Miskito from Nicaragua crossed into Honduras and made his way to Roatán, where he was adopted by an English-speaking family with the surname Bodden (one of the English-blooded Caymanians, no doubt). He took their name and brought it back to the mainland when he left the islands to work for the United Fruit Company in Puerto Castilla (near Trujillo). In the late 1950s he returned to his native land, the Mosquitia, met his wife and stayed, founding the community of Raistá, whose 180 residents today are nearly all descendants. During our 2009 visit to Raistá, community founder William Bodden was still alive, and estimated to be 106 or 107 years old.

---

Snack, Sex with the Captain), and a number of cocktails. The large, multicolored bar, driftwood lounge, and dockside tables always host a crowd of tourists and locals and the music is a quality mix of rock, reggae, and nostalgic '70s and '80s tunes.

Another popular spot, with a bit more of a party, electronica vibe, is **Coco Loco Bar** (4 P.M.–midnight Sun.–Thurs., 4 P.M.–1 A.M. Fri.–Sat.), two doors away—another laid-back oceanfront place to chill out with some tunes and a drink. Happy hour, at sunset, features two-for-one drinks.

One unusually located drinking establishment is **Treetanic Bar** (4 P.M.–midnight daily), literally a treehouse bar in the shape of a boat, very creatively designed and decorated in the canopy of a mango tree to the side of the Jade Seahorse restaurant. The cocktails are a bit more expensive than at other bars but are exceptional, and the surroundings are unbeatable—an elevated walkway leads off the bar, meandering above the creatively landscaped grounds, to a couple of semiprivate seating areas, all like something out of a Dr. Seuss book.

Not quite as unusual, but still very charming is **Babalú** (4 P.M. onwards daily), Utila's oldest dock bar newly revamped. Run by Italian expat Dado, the bar is smaller than Tranquila or Coco Loco, with weathered wood, oars hanging from the ceiling, and oil lamps. Only two kinds of beer (US$1.20) are offered, along with well drinks (US$1.50), but at these rock-bottom prices, who's complaining? A simple and inexpensive menu is available as well, if you are looking for some munchies with your drink.

Over in Sandy Point, **Driftwood Café** has a relaxed bar scene with a mix of expats and locals (some of whom are known to play raucous dice games). The house specialty is Monkey Balls shooters, of vodka and house-made kahlua.

Farther along, **La Champa** (tel. 504/425-3893, noon–midnight Wed. and Sat. nights only, and Sun. during the day) is a huge bamboo and thatch-roof restaurant and bar decorated with wild orchids right on Chepes Beach. They play mellow music, sometimes live, and attract a laid-back, mostly expat crowd. Besides the full bar, they have an extensive menu of fajitas, quesadillas, burgers, and the like for US$3–6 a plate. Their "shuttle service," a multicolored golf cart, will transport customers to and from town (about a 10-minute walk).

The billiard aficionado can find two small **pool halls,** on Cola de Mico across from the Jade Seahorse, although they are usually the exclusive domain of Honduran mainlanders. Both are best visited early as the crowd can get a little rough later on. Beer is served.

Late-night incidents walking home after a night at the bars were once a problem, but locals have pretty much stopped it entirely by instituting "tourist police" who patrol at night, with radios to call regular police. Nonetheless, it's not a bad idea to walk home in groups.

**Reef Cinema** shows several movies a week in a well-designed theater, at 7:30 P.M.

## Shopping

**Bay Island Originals** (tel. 504/425-3372, 9 A.M.–noon and 2–6 P.M. Mon.–Fri., 9 A.M.–noon Sat.) sells locally designed T-shirts, Honduran coffee and cigars, and a variety of better quality tourist collectibles as well as the usual junk. Swimsuits and sunglasses are also available here, if yours have been forgotten at home.

Local character of note Gunter, a German who has lived on the island for many years and who started (but since retired from) the dive shop bearing his name, now dedicates much of his time to sculpture and painting, many works created with natural materials like driftwood found on the beach. Gunter's latest thing is "resin" art, using resin to make different pieces (like shells) appear to float, in an attempt to capture the feel of the underwater world. He also makes jewelry. He shows (and sells) his works at **Gunter's Driftwood Gallery** (tel. 504/425-3113), in his house just off Cola de Mico Road. The best time to visit is in the afternoon, or better yet, call first to make sure he's home.

Another great place to buy art is at **L'Atelier** (tel. 504/3254-6808, 11 A.M.–6 P.M. Mon.–Sat.), the workshop of Argentinian transplant Patricia Suarez. Prices of her abstract paintings are based on size, and a steal considering the quality, starting at just US$10 for a postcard-sized painting and going up to US$500 for a large canvas.

One place in town with a very good selection of used books for sale or exchange is **Funkytown,** on the ground floor of the Reef Cinema (9 A.M.–7:30 P.M. Mon.–Sat.), from classics to beach trash to foreign language.

## ACCOMMODATIONS

In keeping with its status as the least expensive Bay Island, Utila has a plethora of budget rooms for the backpacker crowd, most about US$6–15 d. In recent years the range of rooms has broadened, with several new midrange places and a few higher-end (though still decidedly low-key) resorts. Most of the hotels are in small, wooden buildings, often converted houses, so their proliferation is not visually overwhelming.

One tip for divers: All the dive shops have either lodges or affiliations with hotels and offer free accommodation with a beginner's Open Water certification course, or discounted with other courses or fun dives, typically US$3–5. Although many local families who own small hotels have been put into a difficult situation because of this, it suits budget travelers just fine. All rent out rooms to nondivers as well.

When inquiring at hotels, one important question is whether the establishment has hot water or not. While hot showers may not normally be a question of great importance to some travelers, they can be awfully pleasurable after a day of scuba diving, especially in the rainy season when it's cooler.

Note that while check-out time on the mainland is typically noon, on Utila it's usually 10 A.M.

### Under US$10

In addition to the hotels listed, some pricier hotels (such as Mango Inn and Trudy's Hotel) also have dorm rooms for US$10 or under.

The price that can't be beat is at **Harbour View Hotel** (tel. 504/425-3772, tatiana luna22@yahoo.com), where rooms rent for the bargain basement price of US$2 per person. While the bathrooms are shared, and the water is cold, the place is clean enough, and conveniently shares the pier with a couple of the most popular establishments in town, Tranquila bar and Indian Wok restaurant. Harbour View is affiliated with Parrots Dive Center and gives priority to divers and nondiving friends who are accompanying them.

Another good deal is **Loma Vista** (tel. 504/425-3243, US$7 pp), with clean, sunny rooms with communal kitchen facilities (sink and burners, but no fridge) and a porch with a picnic table and hammock.

The simple rooms at **Monkey Tail Inn** (tel. 504/425-3155, US$5.25 pp) are in need of a paint job, but there's a small porch and wireless Internet throughout the hotel, and it's also home to Cyber Monkey Internet café. It's acceptably clean, although flip-flops are recommended for the concrete cold-water showers.

## US$10-25

**Cooper's Inn** (tel. 504/425-3184, www.coopers-inn.com, US$10 s, US$13 d), past Rubi's on the other side of the road, has clean, well-maintained rooms with fans and mosquito nets, shared bathroom (cold-water only), and access to a shared kitchen, though guests are likely to be tempted by the excellent dinners served in front at Delany's Island Kitchen. The inn is conveniently close to several of the dive shops, for those out-of-bed-into-the-dive-boat mornings. Owner Carissa Cooper is a native Utilian, and a good source of information about the island.

**Freddy's Place** (tel. 504/425-3819, FreddysPlace@gmail.com, US$16 s/d, US$35 with a/c), just over the bridge going toward Bando Beach from downtown, rents the rooms in four two-bedroom apartments with fans. If you rent only one bedroom, you may share the rest of the apartment with another guest; a group that rents both bedrooms will obviously have the whole apartment for themselves. The owner, Fred, a retired fisherman who lived for years in Alaska, is a genial character. Low-season and long-term rates are available. The

building is in a quiet part of town, with a wrap-around deck facing the canal.

Located above the owner's home, the rooms at **Hotel Bavaria** (tel. 504/425-3809, petra whitefield3@hotmail.com, US$13 s, US$16 d) are simple and clean, and just a short walk up Cola de Mico Road. Each has a fan and private bath (cold water only), and they share a porch.

If you want to stay closer to the beach, consider **Margaritaville** (tel. 504/425-3366, US$20 s/d with fan, or US$40 with a/c), opposite Driftwood Café. The 16 breezy, spacious rooms are fairly basic, but each has a clean, tile-floor bathroom, and some have a kitchenette. The hotel's deck affords views of both the harbor and lagoon.

Next to the Utila Lodge, near the Bay Island College of Diving, is the motel-style **Hotel Utila** (tel. 504/425-3340, US$17–58), with rooms varying in price depending on the room size and whether it has air-conditioning or a fan. The whole place is a bit dreary. If you're considering springing for air-conditioning, you can get better value rooms elsewhere.

## US$25-50

**◖ Rubi's Inn** (tel. 504/425-3240, US$18 s, US$25 d) on the main road not far from the center of town heading toward the old airport, on the ocean side of the road, offers spotless rooms with private baths and hot water. The pretty garden and cute white house with blue trim hide a much newer property behind: a two-story wooden lodge next to the water. Air-conditioning is available for significantly more, and there is a communal kitchen available, as well as picnic tables for eating your meal or relaxing with a beer. There is one "honeymoon suite" on the second floor with refrigerator, microwave, and private balcony over the water for US$38 d. Laundry service is available to guests and nonguests.

**Relax Inn** (tel. 504/425-3879, US$35 d, US$40 with a/c), across from Camilla's Bakery and close to several dive shops, has four clean, basic rooms in an attractive wood building, each with refrigerator and hot water. There's a small private dock leading off the hotel's porch.

The owners live on the property and are known to invite guests for an excellent home-cooked meal from time to time.

The family-owned **Trudy's Hotel** (tel. 504/425-3103, US$35 s/d with a/c, US$65 suites with TV, mini-fridge, microwave, and a/c) is a fairly new two-story wood building set along the water's edge, although rooms face a patch of sand rather than the water. Funky fish murals are painted on the walls, and Adirondack chairs grace the breezeway, perfect for relaxing after a day of diving. Nondiving hotel guests can ride out with divers for a snorkel at no charge.

Conveniently located right in the center of town is **Hotel Rose** (tel. 504/425-3127, US$16 s, US$26 d with fan, US$5 more with a/c), a decent deal with hot water, fan, and TV, more for air-conditioning. The upstairs terrace has a fine view of the harbor and is a great place to relax in the afternoon and evening.

## US$50-100

The newly renovated 【 **Lighthouse Hotel** (tel. 504/425-3164 www.utilalighthouse.com, US$50 s, US$65 d) is a great addition to Utila's hotel scene. Built on a pier over the water, the rooms are classy, with ivory wood-paneled walls, blonde wood furniture, and sliding glass doors that maximize light. A couple of rooms command spectacular views of the harbor. Amenities include TV, air-conditioning, a sink and microwave, and a wireless Internet hotspot by the hotel office. There are also two smaller rooms in the building that houses the hotel office with four bunks each, for US$40 a night. Native Utilian Owen O'Niel and his Louisiana wife, Thelma Bodden, go out of their way to ensure that each guest has a wonderful visit to the island.

**Colibri Hill Resort** (tel. 504/425-3329, www.colibri-hotel.com, US$45 s, US$50 d, US$10 off during low season) is a bit of a mixed bag. Really simply a hotel rather than a resort, the property does have a small swimming pool, and a three-story building with attractive rooms for reasonable prices. Details, however, are often overlooked; at our visit the shower curtain was moldy, and a window shade was missing from one of the guest rooms. Although it's only 10 minutes from the center of town, the last stretch of road can be deserted at night, with the final block down a street without lighting (bring a flashlight!).

Two blocks along Cola de Mico Road, the cabins, buildings, and swimming pool of the **Mango Inn** (tel. 504/425-3335, www .mango-inn.com, US$55–150 depending on the size and furnishings of room, US$5–20 off during low season) are set in a lush garden, with palm trees and flowers lining brick paths. The cabins are very nice, with tasteful decorations and details like purified water and a coffee maker in the room. The deluxe and standard rooms are a little older, but still pleasant. A few rooms have been converted into dorms, which can fill with divers from Utila Dive Centre, but if there's a space free, it goes for US$10 a night. The shared bathrooms have cold water only, at least for now, but they're clean, as are the dorms, and it's the only dorm with access to a pool. The restaurant, Mango Café, is run by an Italian expat and serves pizza and pasta, among other things.

A most exceptional array of accommodations, certainly out of the ordinary, is found at 【 **Nightland Cabins at Jade Seahorse** (tel. 504/425-3270, www.jadeseahorse.com, US$100 s/d, US$25 off during low season), located behind the Jade Seahorse restaurant on Cola de Mico Road. Six fantastical cabins with twisted roofs, multicolored windows, carved wood accents, and mosaics in every nook and cranny are tucked into a tropical garden with various octagonal wooden decks, mosaic archways, brick and wood bridges, and gazebos with seating areas. All the rooms have a different color scheme and theme (Shangrila, Mona Lisa, Cama Sutra, Dalai Lama). One of the cabins even has a rooftop porch with views out to the sea. All come with air-conditioning, hot water, refrigerator, and (essential in the rainy season) umbrella.

## Dive Resorts

The best-established dive resort in Utila is **The Utila Lodge** (tel. 504/425-3143, U.S.

tel. 800/282-8932, www.utilalodge.com, dive packages are US$1,100–1,275 per week depending on the season, double occupancy, or US$87/night, room only). The lodge, run by Americans Jim and Kisty Engel, occupies the dark-wood building next to the Bay Islands College of Diving, which is its partner dive shop. It has its own dock for fishing boats and dive boats, as well as eight slightly dated but nice rooms with TV, air-conditioning, and private balconies. Rates include three good cafeteria-style meals and three boat dives daily. Nondivers pay US$985–1,159 a week. Jim is an avid fisherman and will arrange flats or deep-sea fishing trips for guests. The hotel has use of the BICD's small swimming pool and hot tub, free Internet for guests, a bar over the water, a sundeck, and a pool table. The max number of guests is 16, with a full-time staff of 10. The restaurant is open to nonguests as well, and the bar and dock are great spots to watch the sunset.

On the south side of the island and the west side of the canal is **(( Laguna Beach Resort** (tel./fax 504/425-3264, U.S. tel. 800/668-8452, www.lagunabeachresort.info, US$1,465–1,495 pp double occupancy for a seven-night package, or US$225–230 pp/night, with discounts for nondivers and low-season, and surcharges for single occupancy). Packages include dives, meals, snorkeling, horseback riding, and use of kayaks and bicycles. The locally owned resort (same owners as Utila Water Sports) offers 13 bungalows with air-conditioning and a two-bedroom beach house, all set on a private sandy peninsula accessible only by boat. Rooms are not luxurious, but attractive with polished wood floors, and each bungalow has a small dock that leads out into the water. It's a wonderful spot if you're looking for a secluded place to forget about the world for a while. Swimming and snorkeling are fantastic right off the beach out front, and there is a large swimming pool for those who prefer fresh water. Flats and deep-sea fishing on one of their three fishing boats, windsurfing, and sea-kayaking trips are available, and shore diving is unlimited. Trips to town are regularly

available. Equipment is top-notch, and the dive boats are very well-maintained.

**(( Utopia Village** (tel. 504/3344-9387, www.utopiadivevillage.com) is without a doubt the fanciest digs on the island. Owned by a group of partners from the U.S., U.K., and Canada, Utopia is another secluded, all-inclusive resort, with its own private beach. High season rates range US$1,717–1,972 for seven-night dive packages, and fishing and spa/romance packages are available as well, with special rates available for shorter stays. Rooms are elegant, with polished wood floors, good quality linens, and accents in woven rattan and stone. Facilities include a gourmet restaurant on-site, a full-service spa, and of course, a dive center. Basic packages do not include as many services as at Laguna Beach, but can be customized. No children under the age of 15 are allowed. The PADI Open Water certification course is a whopping US$450, but Advanced Open Water is a more standard US$275.

**Deep Blue Resort** (tel. 504/9834-4399, www.deepblueutila.com) is run by a British family, also located on a lagoon accessible only by boat. The rooms are nothing fancy, nor is the food, and admittedly the aging dive boat is a bit slow when heading around the island to dive sites on the revered northern coast. That said, overall it's a pleasant place to stay, and guests rave about the dive masters, and diving is what you came for, isn't it? Rates range US$1,014–1,878 for a seven-night dive package, double occupancy.

There are a couple of much cheaper places that describe themselves as dive resorts, but there's some truth to the maxim "you get what you pay for." Accommodations are basic, and service can be a mixed bag. Better midrange options can be had by arranging your own accommodations at a place like Lighthouse, Trudy's Hotel, or Mango Inn, and choosing your dive shop separately.

Certainly Utila's most unique opportunity, the *Utila Aggressor* (www.aggressor.com) is a live-aboard yacht that can accommodate up to 14 guests. One of a worldwide chain of live-aboard dive yachts, it is (as of the time of writing) the least expensive *Aggressor* in the world, offering five-star accommodation on board for a "mere" US$2,200 per person for a week. It is also perhaps the smallest *Aggressor*—be prepared for tight quarters.

## Apartments

With so many travelers finding themselves transfixed by Utila's reefs and low-key lifestyle, plenty of apartments are up for rent. Prices can range anywhere from US$200–600, depending on what kind of place you're looking for, but average places go for US$400–500 a month for a one-bedroom. Among the **hotels offering long-term rentals** are Cooper's Inn (US$400/month for a one-bedroom, US$550/month for a two-bedroom) as well as Freddy's Place and Countryside Inn.

**Bananaville Apartments** (tel. 504/3369-2298, rm.paradisecove@gmail.com) is one recommended lodging, in a residential area roughly 15 minutes walk from the municipal dock. The one-bedroom apartments rent for US$500 per month, and two single beds can be added to squeeze in four people if needed. Monthly renters are preferred, but weekly renters are considered based on availability, at the rate of US$150 per week. **Sandstone Apartments** (tel. 504/425-3692), out on the point, offers rentals for US$450–800 per month, while a one-bedroom at the newly constructed **Caribbean Dreams** is US$450 a month. Many other places can be found by asking around, particularly through dive masters and instructors, or on www.aboututila.com.

## FOOD

Travelers will be pleased to hear that they can feed themselves on some excellent food in Utila, and for reasonable prices, due to the high competition and also large number of creative cooks, both islander and expat. You'll find everything from tasty *baleada* snacks to great pizza and fried chicken to superlative seafood prepared in all sorts of inventive ways, generally in large, diver-friendly portions.

Restaurants in Utila are all fairly casual, in keeping with the diver/backpacker clientele, and don't take reservations. You may also find yourself spending a lot of time at restaurants, because service on the island tends to be rather relaxed. Those in a hurry might consider buying ready-made sandwiches and snacks at the several bakeries in town, or going to Mermaid's buffet.

## Breakfasts and Baked Goods

**◖ Thompson's Café and Bakery** (6 A.M.–8 P.M. Mon.–Sat., 6 A.M.–2 P.M. Sun.), on Cola de Mico Road not far from the main intersection, sells utterly fantastic and inexpensive breakfasts. It's always packed with divers stuffing themselves with pancakes, omelets, and the famous johnnycake (biscuits served plain or like a McDonald's Egg McMuffin) and washing it all down with a mug of surprisingly good coffee before running out to their 7:30 A.M. dive. Delectable coconut bread and cinnamon rolls are sold to go, and lunch and dinner are available as well. Burgers, biscuits, *baleadas,* and *burritas* are US$0.65–2, while breakfast and dinner plates (*comida típica* as well as items like pork chops) are about US$3.75.

**Munchies** (tel. 504/425-3168, 7 A.M.–5 P.M. Mon.–Sat.), on the first floor of a rambling wooden house just west of the dock on Main Street, serves up a solid breakfast with eggs, bacon, hash browns, juice, and strong coffee for US$4 (available all day). It also has sandwiches and salads. The front porch is a fine spot to greet the day and watch the town amble by.

Next to Bush's Supermarket, **GB's** (6:30 A.M.–2 P.M. daily) has a small selection of English tea, scones, meat pies, and toast with toppings like Nutella and Marmite. The iced coffee is tasty, and a light breakfast will only set you back US$2–3.

A bit farther east is **Camilla's Bakery** (8:30 A.M.–2 P.M. Mon.–Fri.), set back from the road in the pink building just before Zanzibar, serving freshly baked croissants, bagels, and baguettes as well as cakes, muffins, and cinnamon rolls. For a quick lunch, stop in for a ready-made ham-and-cheese croissant.

**Zanzibar's** is a good spot for breakfast, with fluffy pancakes and great smoothies (about US$4), and is open at lunch as well, serving subs and the like.

## Honduran

A few steps beyond Rubi's Inn, on the opposite side of the street, is a white shack run by **Doña Sergia,** serving up fresh juices, snacks, and meals such as *baleadas,* tamales, tacos, pork chops, pasta, and even a vegetarian plate. There's nowhere to sit, but at these prices (US$1–4), who's complaining? You can even book a massage with Doña Sergia for the rock-bottom price of US$10 (for 30 minutes).

If you're not in the mood to sit around waiting for your meal, try the buffet at locally owned **Mermaid's** (tel. 504/425-3395, 11 A.M.–10 P.M. Sun.–Thurs., 11 A.M.–3 P.M. Fri. and 6–10 P.M. Sat.), on the Point, east of the municipal dock. Offerings include creamy mashed potatoes, fried rice, baked potatoes, fried chicken, BBQ chicken, meatballs, and fried fish balls. Combo plates, including drinks, cost US$4–5. There's an open-air seating area, plus a room with air-conditioning—perhaps the only air-conditioned dining on the island. There's also an attached Internet café.

**Big Mamma's** (6 A.M.–3 P.M. Mon.–Sat.), opposite Cross Creek, serves popular inexpensive (US$3.50) daily specials in a bright green restaurant with a nautical theme, but unfortunately the quality is inconsistent.

## Seafood and Meats

Locally owned **[ RJ's Barbecue** (6–9:30 P.M. Wed., Fri., and Sun.), just before the bridge toward the old airport, serves up enormous portions of fresh fish, frequently snapper and tuna, thick steaks, and chicken. Go early as the small restaurant fills up fast and has been known to run out of food.

Also locally owned, **Seven Seas Restaurant** (tel. 504/425-7377, 8 A.M.–10 P.M., closed Sun. and Tues.), on the point across from Utila Water Sports, serves fresh seafood, good fried chicken, inexpensive *baleadas,* burgers, and delicious pork specials. A *baleada* will set you back US$0.60–1.30, while burgers and other meals run US$3–8.50.

On the third floor of the corner building at the municipal dock is locally owned **La Pirata** (tel. 504/425-3988, noon–10 P.M.

daily), serving snacks and light meals (US$3–10) such as ceviche, chicken wings, and burgers, as well as bigger indulgences such as lobster and T-bone steaks (most meals US$6–13, except the lobster, which goes for US$26). There is a nice outdoor deck with nice views across the town and harbor.

Over in Sandy Bay, Texas transplants Bruce and Sharon specialize in smoked meats and crispy beer-battered seafood at their **[ Driftwood Café** (11 A.M.–10 P.M. daily). Sandwiches and burgers run US$4–7, while seafood dishes and meats from the grill are US$7–10. The restaurant is built out over the water and offers a spectacular view with its meals. Alternatively, come here for a sunset drink—which after a couple shooters of Monkey Balls (vodka and housemade kahlua) may turn into a long and lovely evening at the bar.

## International

One of the best restaurants on the island just got better: San Francisco chef and long-time Utila resident Dave Ayarra took over The Island Café. **[ Dave's Island Café** (6:30–9:30 P.M. Tues.–Sat.) is next to Coco Loco Bar. The menu changes daily, and might include barracuda fillet in mango-chili sauce or masala chicken curry, and there is always a creative vegetarian option (a relief if you've been eating nothing but rice and beans during your Honduras visit). Main dishes run about US$5–7.

Utilian-owned **El Picante** (noon–2 P.M. and 4–10 P.M. Sun.–Thurs., 6–10 P.M. Sat.) serves up tasty fajitas and other Mexican standards.

Perhaps the best addition to Utila's dining scene is **[ Indian Wok** (tel. 504/3325-1934, 6 P.M. onwards Sun.–Thurs., although possibly changing to Mon.–Sat. in the future), located on the same pier as Tranquila Bar and Parrots Dive Center. It's run by Canadians Shawn Thompson and Christine Peach, and the daily-changing menu has dishes from around Asia. There are usually both Indian and Thai curries, sushi rolls, and often the very popular Vietnamese spring rolls. Lighting is low, and the ambiance features soft music, candles, and cloth tablecloths. Prices range US$8–11 for oversized portions, and half portions are available for as little as US$4.

Popular with travelers is **Bundu Café** (tel. 504/425-3557, 8 A.M.–2:30 P.M. and 5–9:30 P.M. Fri.–Tues.) on Main Street just east of the center of town, serving crepe and waffle breakfasts, panini and salad lunches, and uncommon dinner dishes such as "beer con chicken" and deep-dish pizza (breakfasts US$3.50–5, lunch and dinner US$5–12).

Built out over the water, **Mariposa Café** (tel. 504/9754-9957, 11 A.M.–10 P.M.) is one of the prettiest places in Utila for a meal. The chef focuses on sourcing local meats, seafood, poultry, and seafood, and they have a wood-burning oven for making their own breads (not to mention pizzas). While the café was temporarily closed during our low-season visit (everyone deserves a vacation sometime, we suppose), it's reader-recommended. Main dishes average US$5–10.

An unusual find on Utila, started by a transplanted Israeli and now run by an Utila woman who worked with him, is **Ultra Light Café** (tel. 504/425-3201, 7 A.M.–10 P.M. Sun.–Fri.) in Sandy Bay, with low-priced and healthy Middle Eastern–style food, such as falafel, hummus, and *zlabia*.

The burritos (US$4) at funky and fun **Skidrow's** (6–9 P.M.) in Sandy Bay (opposite EcoMarine Dive Shop) are huge and filling. Come by on Mondays for a raucous Pub Quiz, popular with the expats.

## Italian

**La Piccola – Kate's Italian Cuisine** (tel. 504/425-3746, 5–10 P.M. Wed.–Sun.), on Main Street west of the dock, is managed by Kate, an Italian expat who makes her own ravioli and gnocchi, and several types of very good sauces, such as the *vesuviana*, of olives, capers, and tomatoes. She also offers imported beef and fresh fish entrées. Much of the seating is on an outdoor terrace, surrounded by a pretty wood trellis with winding flower vines, while indoors is painted in warm cream and rust tones with a cute wine bar (with a decent selection of wines) in the center. It's a bit more upscale than most in Utila, with cloth tablecloths and candles, not to mention good service, but still relaxed. Spaghetti "backpacker specials" are about US$5, while the other dishes are in the US$7–16 range.

**Mango Café** (tel. 504/425-3326, 6:30 A.M.–9:30 P.M. daily), located at the Mango Inn, serves a variety of entrées, including fresh fish and lasagna, as well as well-loved brick-oven pizzas. Although expensive for their size (US$7.50–11 for a pie that feeds one hungry person or two not-so-hungry people), the pizzas have tasty toppings and crispy crusts.

**Delany's Island Kitchen** (tel. 504/425-3184, 5:30–10 P.M., closed Wed. and Sun.) is managed by Delany's daughter Carissa, offering generously portioned lasagna and superb pizza, as well as delicious fish in a creamy garlic-lemon sauce. Locals love to pick up a pie for take-out—not a bad idea if your hotel has a deck with a sunset view, although the hanging rice paper lanterns and strands of colored lights lend the seating area some night-time charm. A meal here will set you back US$6–9.

**Pizza Nut** at Coco Loco Bar is another popular place to grab a pie.

## Groceries

Several stores in town sell fresh produce, cheese, milk, and other perishables, stocked by thrice-weekly shipments from the mainland. Most are open Monday–Saturday only. **Bush's Supermarket** (tel. 504/425-3147, 6:30 A.M.–6 P.M. Mon.–Sat., 6:30 A.M.–noon Sun.) offers the biggest variety of food and the cleanest facilities on the island, and is also one of the few stores open on Sunday. **Samantha's 7-11**, across from the fire station on the way to Sandy Bay, is useful because it stays open until 11 P.M., but selection is limited and prices are on the high side.

A good meat market, though on the small side, is **JB Carnicería** (tel. 504/425-3671, 7 A.M.–noon and 2–6 P.M. Mon.–Sat., 7 A.M.–noon Sun.), with fresh seafood and meat (including beef, pork, chicken) daily.

# INFORMATION AND SERVICES

## Research Centers and Volunteering

There is a surprising number of volunteer opportunities on Utila with local research centers dedicated to the local flora and fauna. All are flexible with schedules to enable you to take diving courses or Spanish lessons during your stay as well.

One- to three-month stays as research assistants or environmental educators are available with the **Bay Island Conservation Society** (tel. 504/425-3260, www.bicautila.org, 8 A.M.–noon and 2–5 P.M. Mon.–Fri.). The visitors center, a 15-minute walk out of town, up Cola de Mico Road heading toward the airport, has pamphlets, maps, and books on Utila and the Bay Islands. The center is also the office of the Turtle Harbour Wildlife Refuge and Marine Reserve. A one-month program is $350, including accommodation, electricity, Internet, water, and laundry.

The **Whale Shark & Oceanic Research Centre** (tel. 504/425-3760, www.wsorc.com) conducts whale shark monitoring and research year-round, and works to raise public awareness about marine conservation. They offer four-hour whale shark encounter trips for US$44 that include the snorkel equipment, reef tax, and a short lecture on whale shark ecology. There are also a number of one-day PADI specialty courses such as Whale Shark Awareness and Underwater Naturalist available. For those interested in getting more involved, research volunteers are welcome, as are those interested in fundraising or public education.

The **Iguana Research and Breeding Station** (www.utila-iguana.de, 2–5 P.M. Mon., Wed., and Fri., US$2) makes for an interesting expedition to watch the prehistoric-looking and surprisingly large iguanas feed and wander around. The station has several species of swamp iguana, *Ctemosaura baberi*, found only in the mangrove swamps of Utila and in danger of extinction due to overhunting and the cutting of the mangroves. The volunteers are extremely knowledgeable. They offer a few

guided tours on the island, such as an "ironbound tour" through tropical forest to volcanic-rock formations on north shore, US$8 per person. Call or email in advance to arrange a tour.

The **Utila Centre for Marine Ecology** (tel. 504/425-3026, www.utilaecology.org) has six principle areas of research: megafauna (dolphins, orcas, and whale sharks), reef fisheries, coral reef ecology, mangrove systems, seagrass ecology, and island ecology. UCME frequently works with students completing research for undergraduate and post-grad theses. Volunteer stays start at US$1,025 for two weeks and go up to US$3,250 for eight weeks. Volunteers must have PADI Advanced Open Water certification, but specialty research diver training is included in the volunteer program.

## Travel Agencies

One very good travel agency on the island is **Worldwide Travel** (tel. 504/425-3394, aliceww travel@yahoo.com, 9 A.M.–4:30 P.M. Mon.–Sat.), located on Losano Road (which is the road that turns left at the Mango Inn) and run by extremely efficient and accommodating Utilian Alice Gabourel. She can book domestic and international flights as well as hotel rooms and car rentals.

## Banks

Both **HSBC** and **Banco Atlántida** (8–11:30 A.M. and 1:30–4 P.M. Mon.–Fri., 8–11:30 A.M. Sat.) change travelers checks and dollars, and both have ATMs (although Banco Atlántida's only works with Visa cards). There is also an ATM at Mermaid's restaurant. Several spots in town will give cash advances on MasterCard, Visa, and AmEx, typically charging a 7 percent commission, including at **Rivera's Supermarket** (7 A.M.–8 P.M. Mon.–Sat., 7 A.M.–6 P.M. Sun.).

## Communications

**Hondutel** is in Sandy Bay, next to the police station. Also, there's the **Utila Telephone Co.** (8 A.M.–8 P.M. daily), across the street from Hondutel. **Honducor** (tel. 504/425-3167,

8 A.M.–3:55 P.M. Mon.–Fri., 9 A.M.–11:55 A.M. Sat.) is right on the dock.

Internet service is easily available in Utila, usually by the minute. On the main road in the large building at the corner with the dock is **San Fernando Wireless** (8 A.M.–9 P.M. Mon.–Sat., 8 A.M.–6 P.M. Sun.), charging US$2 an hour. Opposite Banco Atlántida is a little joint that charges only US$1.50 per hour.

The Internet café at **Mermaid's** restaurant (9 A.M.–10 P.M. Sun.–Thurs., 9 A.M.–5 P.M. Fri., 6–10 P.M. Sat.) has good air-conditioning and charges US$2.40 per hour for the Internet and US$0.11 per minute for calls to the United States.

**Cyber Monkey,** a small Internet café located at the Monkey Tail Inn on Cola de Mico Road, offers Internet and Skype for US$0.80 per 15 minutes or US$2.40 per hour.

Many of the Internet cafés can make wallet-size photos, required for each PADI course, US$0.50 each.

## Laundry

There seem to be a million and one places offering laundry service on Utila. Prices are around US$4 for a large bag of dirty clothes. One option is **Alice's Laundry** (7 A.M.–8 P.M. daily), which also has an Internet café on the premises (8:30 A.M.–8 P.M. daily), charging US$2.60 to wash a large grocery bag of clothes.

## Spanish School

Although English is more widely spoken on Utila than Spanish, the **Central American Spanish School** (tel. 504/425-3788, www.ca-spanish.com) offers popular and recommended Spanish classes on Utila for US$150 a week for 20 hours of private classes or US$100 for 20 hours of group classes (discounts are often available for the private classes). CASS has its main office in La Ceiba, with offices in Roatán, and Copán Ruinas as well, and can arrange monthlong programs combining a week on Utila with a dive course, two weeks of classes, and a homestay in La Ceiba, and a week of classes and homestay in Copán. It is east of the municipal dock opposite the water.

## Emergencies

In an emergency, contact the **police** (tel. 504/425-3145 or after hours at 504/425-3187).

The **Utila Medical Store** (tel. 504/425-3400, 8 A.M.–8 P.M. Mon.–Sat.), east of the dock on the water side, sells medications and also does laboratory analysis (urine, blood tests, etc.). For a doctor's advice, visit the **Utila Community Clinic** (8 A.M.–noon Mon.–Fri.), opposite the Mizpah Methodist church, which charges just a few dollars. It's best to get there at 7 A.M., since the wait can be incredibly long and the earlier you arrive, the closer you are to the front of the line.

In the unlikely event of a decompression problem during a dive, your dive shop should take you post-haste to the **hyperbaric chamber** at the Bay Islands College of Diving (tel. 504/425-3378, VHF channel 71, 8:30 A.M.–3:30 P.M. Mon.–Sat., and 24 hours in an emergency).

## Immigration

The *migración* office is on the main dock in town. At the time of writing immigration officials had been instructed to automatically give tourists 90-day visas, and renewal of any oddly shorter visas had to be taken care of in Tegucigalpa.

## GETTING THERE AND AWAY
### Air

**Sosa** has flights to Utila from La Ceiba Monday–Saturday, and might also have Sunday flights during the March–August high season. Sosa tickets are sold by the dock, at **Morgan's Travel** (tel. 504/425-3161, U.S. tel. 786/623-4167, utilamorganstravel@yahoo.com, 8 A.M.–noon and 2–5 P.M. Mon.–Sat.), in the blue wooden building across from the ferry office. Morgan's can also book international flights.

If you are arriving on an international flight from the United States that connects in San Pedro Sula and La Ceiba, it is highly recommended to check your luggage only as far as San Pedro. Hoteliers in Utila report many cases of luggage that doesn't make the connection—better to retrieve it in San Pedro and get it onto the next flight yourself.

Utila's airstrip on the north side of the island is four kilometers from downtown, following Cola de Mico Road. You *must* reconfirm your flight at the Sosa office the day before your flight. They have a shuttle bus driver who will pick you up and take you to the airport for US$2 per person. Be waiting outside of your hotel promptly at the appointed time—the driver has been known to simply drive on by if the guest is not outside. Taxis meet regularly scheduled flights, charging the same price back into town.

Sosa sometimes offers charter service (particularly during high season, or anytime if you traveling in a group of seven or more), and Morgan's Travel might have information about other charter services. If Utilian native Troy Bodden isn't using his personal plane, he also allows it to be chartered (tel. 504/425-3264 or 504/9869-8972, ask for Claudia). Trips from Utila to Roatán or La Ceiba cost US$300 for 3–5 passengers, depending on the quantity of luggage. If you are arriving by charter flight, be sure to arrange a pickup with your hotel or with Paisano's Taxis, or there won't be anyone around to take you into town. Likewise, if you are departing by charter, you might want to tip your taxi driver to stick around until after your flight has actually taken off.

*Note:* When visibility is poor on the north coast due to bad weather (not uncommon for much of the year), the airport at La Ceiba closes with regularity. Don't be surprised to find yourself stranded if the weather turns bad.

### Boat

The *Utila Princess II* (www.utilaprincess .com) departs Utila for La Ceiba at 6:20 A.M., returns from La Ceiba to Utila daily at 9:30 A.M., departs Utila again at 2 P.M., and departs La Ceiba again at 4 P.M. Departures can vary during the slow season, so check first, especially in La Ceiba where you don't want to take a taxi out to the dock and have to wait around. Travelers can spend the hourlong ride inside or on deck enjoying the breeze. Cost is

US$22 per person, and tickets are sold in the cement building at the entrance to the dock (tel. 504/425-3390). As with air transport, though as not as frequently, the boat is sometimes cancelled due to bad weather. This boat is considerably smaller than the one that travels between La Ceiba and Roatán; if the wind has been blowing and the boat goes anyhow, be prepared for some stomach-turning swells. *Note:* There are often extra trips during Semana Santa, except on Good Friday, when the ferry doesn't run at all.

Captain Rusty (tel. 504/3553-7187) does three-day **charter sailboat trips** from Utila to the Cayos Cochinos, for US$250 per person (minimum two people). Bear in mind that if you do an overnight trip with him, it can be fairly tight quarters on his 40-foot boat. He also does Utila–Roatán trips on his boat for US$50 per person. Captain Hank (tel. 504/3379-1049, sunyata84@hotmail.com) has a 55-foot sloop with three private staterooms, air-conditioning, hot showers, kayaks, and snorkeling (diving, of course, can be arranged), charging US$100 per person for an overnighter to Cayos Cochinos and US$200 per person for two nights/three days. He also offers service between Utila and Roatán, charging US$75 per person for three meals and one night on the boat (four-person minimum). Trips to Belize can also be arranged.

Carissa Cooper and her husband, at Cooper's Inn (tel. 504/425-3184), have a boat, and when the whale sharks are around, they will do two-hour trips with the chance to snorkel (US$50 pp, 2–4 people). They can also help put you in touch with reliable local fishermen for trips to Water Cay (US$37 for up to four people).

For more information on local boating, contact the port captain's office (tel. 504/425-3116) by the dock.

## GETTING AROUND

**Lance Bodden Rentals** (tel. 504/425-3245, boddenlance@yahoo.com) rents scooters, ATVs, and motorcycles for US$40–70 a day, including gas. Bicycles are available for US$5 a day.

**Rita's Boutique** (tel. 504/425-3692) also rents golf carts: US$40 for six hours, US$50 for eight hours, and US$280/week.

**Delco Bike Rentals,** just west of the dock on Main Street, rents out fairly sturdy mountain bikes at US$5 a day. Slightly more abused bikes are available for a bit less, and rates drop for multiday rentals. Another rental shop is **Utila Bike Rentals,** also on Main Street, past Bush's supermarket on the left, charging US$3 a day, less per week and month.

If you should need a taxi for any reason, call **Paisano's Taxi Service** (tel. 504/425-3311) 24 hours a day. It's based out of a little grocery of the same name.

# ◖ UTILA CAYS

The Utila Cays are a collection of 12 tiny islets off the southwest corner of the main island.

## Jewel and Pigeon Cays

Some 400 people live on Jewel (or Suc-Suc) Cay and Pigeon Cay, which are connected by a narrow causeway and generally referred to jointly as Pigeon Cay. These islanders are descended from the first residents, who came to Utila from the Cayman Islands in the 1830s. Originally, the migrants settled on the main island but soon moved out to the cays, reputedly to avoid the sand flies, which are much less common than on the main island, especially when the easterly breeze is up. If you found Utila residents to be an odd Caribbean subculture, the Pigeon Cay population is odder still—a small, isolated group who tend to keep to themselves, but nevertheless welcome the occasional visitor with friendly smiles.

At the east end of the causeway on Jewel Cay is the small **Hotel Kayla** (no phone), with simple rooms with private baths (cold water only, US$10 s/d). Check at Captain Morgan's Dive Shop (tel. 504/425-3349, www.diving utila.com) to find out if rooms are available—all the divers from the shop stay there. Another hotel next door (Kayla 2) has similar rooms.

For food, **Susan's Restaurant** is famed for excellent fish burgers and conch stew. It also sells *bando* (an Utilian fish stew) to go, for those on their way to Water Cay. At **Bessie's Fish Factory,** visitors heading out to Water Cay and looking to make a cookout can buy a couple of fresh fish—and if you ask nicely, the proprietors will fillet and season the fish for you. They also sell conch, lobster, and (in season) crab. Food (restaurants and groceries) is cheaper here than on Utila proper, and there are far fewer sand fleas.

## Sandy and Little Cays

Normally an extravagance few can afford, a stay on a **private island** is also possible in the Utila Cays. George Jackson (tel. 504/425-2005 or 504/408-3100, CayosUtila@hotmail .com) rents out **Little Cay** (US$115/night, up to six people) and **Sandy Cay** (US$100/night for a two-bedroom house, up to six people). Each small cay has one house—perfect for a weekend getaway or lounging in the sand and snorkeling the clear, turquoise waters. If some guests don't mind sleeping on mattresses on the living room floor, an additional eight people can be squeezed into the house on Sandy Cay, and countless more can camp out on the beach, while the house and cabin on Little Cay can accommodate up to 12 (US$15 for each additional person). Little Cay is about 5 minutes by boat from Pigeon Cay or 20 minutes from Utila's municipal dock, while Sandy Cay is a bit farther afield. Reservations can also be made through Captain Morgan's Dive Shop (tel./fax 504/425-3349, www.divingutila.com). The cays are heavily booked, so be sure to plan in advance and make a reservation. More information and some photos can be found on the website www.aboututila.com.

## Water Cay

If you were to conjure up the ideal tropical beach paradise, your picture might be something very close to Water Cay. Almost within shouting distance of Pigeon Cay, Water Cay is a patch of sand several hundred meters long, wide at one end and tapering to a point on the other; the only occupants are coconut palms and one small caretaker's shack. Piercingly blue, warm water and a coral reef just a few meters out ring the cay. There are no permanent residents on the island. The caretaker (who shows up most days but doesn't live on the island) collects a US$1.25 entrance fee and also rents hammocks for another US$1 a night, though they're not the finest quality—better to bring your own, or bring a tent. It's also possible to catch a ride on frequent water taxis over to nearby Pigeon Cay for a nominal fee. The best snorkeling is off the south side, though it can be a bit tricky finding an opening in the wall. Water Cay is a popular impromptu party spot for locals and travelers, especially on weekends and on the full moon, which has unfortunately resulted in a bit of trash. Consider taking a plastic bag with you, to carry out a small portion if you can.

To get to Water Cay, check at the Bundu Café, look for any of the brightly painted "charter boat trips" signs around town, ask for Captain Hank next door to Utila Water Sports, or talk to any of the old fishermen hanging out, chatting, or playing dominoes on the stretch of road between Cross Creek and Utila Water Sports. Every August, Water Cay hosts the **Sun Jam** festival, bringing DJs and party-goers out for a wild night of dancing fun (www.sunjamutila.com).

# Guanaja

Guanaja has somehow ended up as the forgotten Bay Island, overlooked in the rush of travelers and migrants to Utila and Roatán. This oversight is surprising considering Guanaja's fantastic reef, wide-open north-side beaches, and quirky fishing towns. News reports have frequently heralded big hotel investments for Guanaja by the wealthy and famous, but tourism on the island continues to be low-key and small-scale dive.

It is possible to survive on the island on a budget, though not as easily as on Utila. This is definitely a more unusual destination, not the mainstream feel of Roatán or the backpacker vibe of Utila, but something else altogether, funky and remote. Big-time tourist development may well hit Guanaja soon, but it hasn't yet.

Christopher Columbus landed here in 1502, on his fourth and final voyage to the Americas. Columbus named it Isla de los Pinos—pines long covered the terrain, but were wiped out in 1998 by the 290-kph winds of Hurricane Mitch. The fishing town of Mangrove Bight was also demolished (miraculously with no deaths), and Savanna Bight and Bonacca were heavily damaged as well. Reforestation projects got underway shortly after the storm passed, and the island cover is coming back. The vast majority of Guanaja's population lives in Bonacca, but there are also sprinklings of people at Mangrove Bight, Savanna Bight, and the post-hurricane town of Mitch, for a total of some 10,000 people.

The sand flies can be thick on Guanaja, so be sure to bring your repellent. The north side has many more than the south—but also the best beaches. Remember that DEET damages the coral, and either rinse off before getting in the water or look for a repellent with natural ingredients.

Guanaja is a diver's paradise. Many divers find the wildlife more varied here than at Roatán, with some very dramatic tunnels and caverns ("better than Mary's Place" claims one diver who has been to both Roatán and Guanaja). Sea life includes black, wire, and gorgonian coral, spotted eagle rays, moray eels, turtles, nurse sharks, lobsters, crabs, and much more.

Many hotels do not have hot water, but showers in the afternoon are typically pleasant, the water having been warmed by the sun.

## BONACCA (GUANAJA TOWN)

Bonacca—officially Guanaja Town, and often just called the Cay—is not actually on the main island, but on one of the cays, and is home to some 6,000 people. It is an architectural

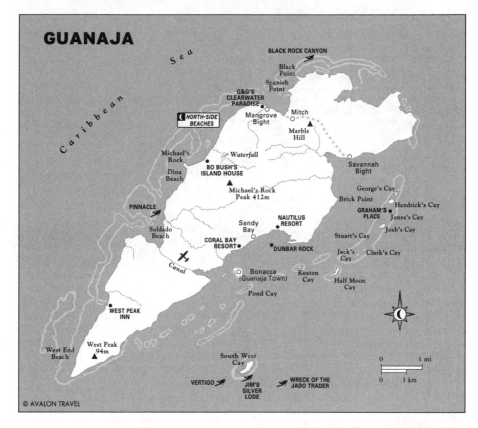

GUANAJA

oddity, built on rickety wooden causeways over a maze of canals, founded in the 1830s by immigrants from the Cayman Islands. They constructed their homes on what were then Hog and Sheen Cays. These two tiny little islets, with a total of one kilometer of land space connected by a shoal, have since been built to cover 18 square kilometers by generations tossing their garbage out the window and eventually covering it over with sand, shells, and coral. With waterways instead of streets, the town is sometimes described as the Venice of the Caribbean (although the similarities begin and end with the canals).

With no beaches or other obvious attractions, Bonacca is worth a visit only to meet the islander townsfolk and take care of any business you might have. Anyone who spends a couple of days wandering the maze of causeways that make up the island will soon make a few acquaintances and start to hear the endlessly entertaining local gossip and tall tales.

Water taxis ply the canals of Bonacca, although within town it's easy to get everywhere by foot.

## ELSEWHERE ON THE ISLAND
### Mangrove Bight

This small fishing village on the northeast corner of Guanaja, formerly perched over the shallow waters of a small bay, had the dubious distinction of being the first inhabited place to come in contact with Hurricane Mitch, at 10 A.M. on October 26, 1998. Luckily, the

© MIKE JONES

Guanaja's main town, Bonacca

storm hit in the morning, so the entire town had time to flee their houses and head up into the surrounding hills, watching as 10-meter waves swept their town away entirely. By 2000, the town had been rebuilt, now located a safe distance away from the shoreline.

Mangrove Bight is populated by a mix of *ladino* and islander families, all dependent on the modest local fishing fleet. Mangrove Bight is usually stroked by a steady breeze, which keeps the sand flies and mosquitoes to a minimum. A couple of *comedores* in town serve up inexpensive eggs, burgers, and other basic meals.

A few points of rock sticking up out in the bay in front of Mangrove Bight indicate the location of the reef. It's a fair swim out but doable for strong snorkelers who keep their eyes peeled for boat traffic. Once to the reef, poke around to find a sufficiently deep opening to pass through, and get ready for a heart-stopping drop-off into the blue depths below on the far side. Visibility is not fantastic and the water is a bit choppy, but the drop-off is a pretty dramatic sight.

### Inland from Mangrove Bight

From Mangrove Bight, a dirt road heads southeast past an unused airstrip and across a low point in the interior of the island to **Savannah Bight,** about an hour away through mosquito-filled pasture land. Rooms are often available for rent in Savannah Bight, which has frequent boat service to Bonacca Town, especially in the mornings.

Not far outside of Mangrove Bight is the town of **Mitch,** a small community that sprang up where some of Mangrove Bight's homeless pitched tents after the 1998 hurricane of the same name.

About halfway between Mangrove Bight and Savannah Bight, you'll pass **Marble Hill,** an anomalous, tree-covered outcrop on the west side of the road. On the far side of the hill is the largest known pre-Columbian ceremonial site on the Bay Islands, **Plan Grande.** The site was mapped in the 1930s before being completely pillaged of its pottery and jade artifacts and destroyed. Little remains of either the ceremonial site or a large residential complex nearby, but locals will take a visitor to poke around for a fee. The Instituto Hondureño de Antropologia e Historia (IHAH) is planning a serious excavation at the site, but moving slowly. The road between Mangrove Bight and Savannah Bight offers good views of the mountains in the center of the island.

For the industrious, a trail leads from the western end of Mangrove Bight up a small valley, over a peak, and down the other side to Sandy Bay, on the south side of the island. The summit of the 412-meter peak is flat and reportedly a good spot for camping. Needless to say, the views from the top are stunning. Fresh water can sometimes be found, but it's best to bring enough for the whole trip, which could be done in a long day. The walk is longer than it may look, due to several high valleys not visible from below that must be crossed.

## North-Side Beaches

Between Mangrove Bight in the east and West End Beach are a series of very fine white-sand beaches, populated only by low-key resort hotels tucked into the edge of the forest. For maximum enjoyment, stay a couple of days out here, either in one of the hotels or camping (bring everything needed, including water). Day trips while staying in either Mangrove

Bight or Bonacca are also feasible. Don't forget to come prepared for sand flies and mosquitoes; they can be fierce on the north side.

About a 45-minute walk west of Mangrove Bight by trail begins a stretch of beautiful beach winding around to **Michael's Rock,** a rocky headland jutting into the ocean. The entire beach is lovely, but the best sections—two stretches of powdery sand and brilliant pale blue water separated by a grove of coconut palms—are right on either side of the headland. Small patches of reef around Michael's Rock offer snorkeling possibilities, but the main reef is over a kilometer offshore.

On the way to Michael's Rock is **Bo Bush's Island House.** Not far from Bo's place, a small creek comes out of the hills, and a trail follows it a half-hour walk uphill to a small waterfall surrounded by lush vegetation.

From Michael's Rock, **Dina Beach** is visible farther southwest, but walking is difficult as the trail passes through thick underbrush in order to bypass rocky coastline. It's better to get dropped off by boat and picked up

© MIKE JONES

Michael's Rock, on the north side of Guanaja

© MIKE JONES

one of Guanaja's waterfalls

later instead of trying to walk from Mangrove Bight. This is a great beach for camping, but there's no fresh water anywhere nearby, so be sure to bring enough.

Southwest of Dina Beach, near the mouth of the canal, is **Soldado Beach,** the reputed site of Columbus's landing in 1502. Nearby is a half-built monument marking the event—Spain donated money for a small museum, but somehow the money didn't go as far as expected. The snorkeling is great here.

**West End Beach,** west past the canal on the north side of the island, is a long stretch of beautiful, virtually unoccupied beach. The only facility in West End is the **West Peak Inn.** A nearby trail ascends to the top of West Peak (94 meters) for views across Guanaja and over to Barbareta and Roatán.

## RECREATION

Guanaja's dive shops are attached to hotels, but they're often willing to take out day divers. Bo Bush, owner of the Island House on Guanaja's north side, will take out day divers at reasonable prices.

Snorkeling right off Bonacca is an unpleasant adventure, as the surrounding coral is dead and litter content in the water is high. It's better to hire a boat and go to the northwest sides of either Southwest Cay or Half Moon Cay, where vibrant corals are found in shallow water.

The enterprising can ask around in Bonacca to set up fishing trips in local waters. Wahoo, king mackerel, and barracuda are frequent catches.

## ENTERTAINMENT

The bars and discos of Guanaja are not for the meek, filled as they are with rough characters who are always ready for a brawl, but they can be a good time if you know how to look after yourself. There are discos in Bonacca, Savanna Bight, and Mangrove Bight. The bars at Bo's and the other resorts can be fun places to spend the evening, and rather more relaxed. The **Pirate's Den Bar** (tel. 504/453-4308, 8 A.M.–2 P.M. and 5:30–9:30 P.M. daily) in Bonacca is a decent place to stop by for a beer in the afternoon.

## ACCOMMODATIONS

The favored lodgings for vacationers on Guanaja are several self-contained beach and dive hotels scattered around the island. On the north side, set on deserted stretches of Caribbean beach, are two great low-key resorts, West Peak Inn and Bo Bush's Island House—the small-scale kind of places that are easy on the environment and perfect for those looking to get away from it all.

Budget travelers can seek out less expensive rooms in Mangrove Bight or Savannah Bight, or camp on the mostly undeveloped north-side beaches.

### Beach Hotels

Situated on a picture-perfect stretch of north-side beach is **( West Peak Inn** (tel. 504/408-3072, U.S. tel. 831/786-0406, www .westpeakinn.com, US$620 pp/week double occupancy, or US$95 pp/night), a collection of rustic but well-equipped cabins (screened-in porches, mosquito nets, fans, private bath) in a low-key and very relaxed setting. Snorkeling,

# TOP DIVE SITES IN GUANAJA

Guanaja may be small, but it boasts 38 moored dive sites – plenty to keep divers busy over a week's time. Novice divers can explore caves and grottoes teeming with colorful marine life, but many of the dives are best suited for more experienced divers. A few of the highlights are:

- **Black Rock Canyon:** This maze of caves and tunnels was created long ago by volcanic activity. There are plenty of silverside sardines, glassy sweepers, groupers, and barracudas. Sharks and moray eels are known to sleep in its nooks and crannies – be sure to bring a dive light.

- *Don Enrique* **Wreck:** The wall here drops 24 meters to a sandy bottom, which slopes down to a sunken shrimp boat, its mast stabbing 15 meters up through the water. Both the wreck and the wall are teeming with sealife, often including spotted eagle rays.

- *Jado Trader:* This is a renowned sunken 60-meter freighter lying on a sandy shelf next to the barrier wall. The maximum depth here is 33 meters. The fish are fed here, and so plenty of grouper and yellowtail hang around, as well as moray eels, horse-eye jacks, and amberjack. Hammerhead sharks

have been spotted at the site. This site is not for novices, and Wreck Certification is recommended for those who want to penetrate where the light does not.

- **Jim's Silverlode:** A tunnel along the wall at a depth of 21 meters brings divers into a sandy-bottomed amphitheater-like area populated by huge groupers, yellowtails, and moray eels. Swarms of silverside sardines keep divers company along the way. This is an intermediate-level dive.

- **The Pinnacle:** Located in a channel, the pinnacle stands on a sandy bottom at 135 feet, rising to a point about 55 feet below the surface. The pinnacle is covered with gorgonian, wire, and black coral, while seahorses, groupers, and spotted drums swim nearby. Divers typically sink to 24 meters and then spiral up and around. The wall of the channel also has beautiful coral at only 3-9 meters deep.

- **Vertigo:** This site along the barrier reef wall has spectacular drop-offs. The top of the wall is at about 11 meters, drops to 49 meters where there is a sandy shelf, then drops off again beyond sight. Black and white sea lilies (crinoids) can be found here.

sea kayaking, and hiking are all available at the lodge, and the restaurant serves up tasty seafood and other plates. (Rates include all meals, unlimited use of sit-on-top kayaks and snorkeling gear, hiking, beachcombing, casual fishing from the dock and shore, and boat transport to and from the Guanaja airstrip.) Some diving is available, but limited to experienced divers—they themselves suggest booking with a dive resort (such as Coral Bay or Bo's) if you're looking for a full week of diving. Rates include three meals a day and free transportation to and from the airport. The owners also can organize multiday sea-kayak and camping trips. The showers lack hot water, but the water is warm in the afternoon if it's been sunny. The entire place runs on energy from solar panels.

The beach hotel **Graham's Place** (tel. 504/3368-5495, U.S. tel. 305/407-1568, www .grahamsplacehonduras.com) charges US$100 per person, which includes breakfast, lunch, and airport transportation, and is a great place to relax on a spectacular beach. There's great snorkeling, including a "natural aquarium"— a large penned-off area in the water where guests can snorkel with fish, turtles, lobsters, and conchs. (Some love it, some hate to see the animals penned.) On land you might spot rabbits, iguanas, and birds. There's bone-fishing right off the cay, and bottom-fishing and trolling can also be arranged. Graham's is located on one of the cays off the southern side of Guanaja; water taxis can easily be arranged for those who are coming just for a meal.

## Dive Resorts

One of the more relaxed, friendly, and less expensive dive hotels in the Bay Islands is **( Bo Bush's Island House** (tel. 504/9963-8551, www.bosislandhouse.com, US$812 pp per diver, US$696 nondiver, daily rates available), built and managed by Bo, who can trace his ancestry back to the time of the English pirates on the island, and his wife. Bo is a bilingual, experienced island diver with more than 6,000 dives under his belt and a fast boat, and he knows a whole world of north-side dive sites, including caverns, walls, reef gardens, wrecks, and more. The comfortable stone-and-wood house set into the hillside can sleep 18, and two small guesthouse another four, but Bo's boat can only handle six divers, which keeps dive size manageable. Rates include all meals, airport transfer, and (for divers) two daily dives. Sea kayaks are available to guests. The isolated hotel on Guanaja's north shore has a positively tranquilizing atmosphere, with wide stretches of deserted beach all around. Bo, a very friendly and laid-back host, will happily take guests on hiking trips and island tours.

At Sandy Bay, on the southern shores of the island, with a narrow 300-meter beach of its own, is **Nautilus Resort,** a 19th-century country house with seven guest rooms. Its sister property, **Dunbar Villa,** is a five-bedroom house dramatically perched atop Dunbar Rock, right in the middle of the bay. Guest rooms are not fancy, but clean and comfortable, and the views are unbeatable. U.S. Dive Travel will arrange San Pedro–Guanaja flights for all guests (U.S. tel. 952/953-4124, www.usdivetravel.com, US$1,505 pp low season, US$1,621 pp high season for a weeklong package, including all meals and dives; flights and tariffs are extra).

At Pelican Reef, not far from Sandy Bay, is the **Coral Bay Dive Resort** (tel. 504/9695-9557, www.coralbay.ca, US$1,169 pp diver, US$1,056 pp nondiver, with discounts available during the low season), also highly recommended. The resort offers a number of classes in addition to regular dives, including Open Water referral for PADI, SSI, NAUI, and ACUC for US$210, or the full Open Water

course for US$375. Nondivers should bear in mind that the resort pool is occasionally in use for dive instruction in the mornings. Nightly rates are US$140–186. They can arrange to pick you up by boat from Roatán, a 90-minute ride, and have plans to work with Rollins Air for transfers from Roatán by air in the future.

Construction was nearing completion at the time of writing at **G&G's Clearwater Paradise** (tel. 504/3303-7444, U.S. tel. 512/452-6990, www.clearwaterparadise.com), a small resort with eight guest rooms near Mangrove Bight. G&G stands for owners George and Ginger—both divers themselves, and Ginger reputedly a fine cook. The hotel restaurant, **Paradise Bar and Grill,** is built out over the water.

## Accommodations in Bonacca and Other Towns

In the middle of Bonacca on the main street is **Hotel Miller** (tel. 504/453-4327, US$19 s, US$22 d with fan and hot water), a large two-story house with rooms on the second floor. There are nicer rooms with air-conditioning and TV for a few dollars more. Rooms are often available for rent in Mangrove Bight or Savannah Bight at around US$10 a night; just ask around.

## FOOD

The resorts include meals, but for those looking to strike out, **( Manati** in Sandy Bay is the place to go, run by a German couple who prepare authentic dishes like weiner schnitzel, as well as delicious island fare, German beer, and a variety of European schnapps. Locals love to while away a Saturday afternoon here, and there is often live music.

The restaurants at Graham's, West Peak Inn, and Bo's are all open to the public, and are great places to visit for a meal if you're not already a guest. The Sunday barbecue at Bo's is another popular gathering spot for resident expats.

One of the better restaurants in Bonacca is **Mexitreats** (8 A.M.–1:30 P.M. and 6–9:30 P.M. Mon.–Fri., 6 A.M.–10 P.M. Sat.–Sun.), owned by a Honduran and his Mexican wife, with inexpensive snacks and light meals like *chilaquiles, baleadas,* nachos, and burgers.

**Commercial Woods** and **Sikaffy's,** both in Bonacca, are the two major grocery stores on the island, although there are plenty of smaller shops and vegetable stands. Friday is the best day for shopping, since the boat comes in with new produce either Thursday afternoon or Friday morning.

## SERVICES
### Banks and Communications
**Banco Atlántida** (tel. 504/453-4262) in Bonacca changes both dollars and travelers checks, and can give a cash advance on a Visa credit card. **Hondutel** (7 A.M.–9 P.M. Mon.– Fri., 7 A.M.–4 P.M. Sat.) is at the south end of the main street.

**Coral Bay Dive Resort** (tel. 504/9695-9557, www.coralbay.ca) near Sandy Bay has an Internet café, with very steep prices: US$7.50 for 15 minutes, US$12 for 30, and US$18 for an hour.

### Boat Mooring
Graham of **Graham's Place** (tel. 504/3368-5495, U.S. tel 305/407-1568, www.grahams placehonduras.com) offers free mooring (up to 45 feet) for **yachts,** fresh water (to fill tank and wash down boat), ice, and laundry service.

### Emergencies
In an emergency, contact the **police** (tel. 504/453-4310); don't light fires because there is no fire department on Guanaja.

## GETTING THERE AND AWAY
**Sosa** (tel. 504/453-4359) flies once daily except Sunday to Guanaja from La Ceiba; **Isleña** (tel. 504/453-4801, www.flyislena.com) flies daily, charging US$52 one-way. The airstrip is on the main island, with no terminal except a simple shelter. Boats always come out to meet the flights and charge a few dollars (depending on current fuel prices) for the 10-minute ride to town. A water taxi out to one of the farther-flung resorts will cost more, perhaps US$25, although transportation can also usually be arranged directly with the hotel. Both airlines have offices in Guanaja where tickets can be purchased.

There has been intermittent ferry service between Guanaja and Trujillo in the past, but in early 2009 it was suspended. There has also been talk of establishing ferry service between La Ceiba and Guanaja, but for the time being that also remains just talk.

## GETTING AROUND
Private boats arrive and depart frequently each day, heading between Bonacca Town and various parts of the main island. Usually islanders arrive in town in the morning, shop or sell goods, and leave again at midday. The only way to find out about them is to just start asking around in Bonacca. A ride to Mangrove Bight, an hour or so away, depending on the size of the outboard, normally costs about US$7 if the boat is already going your way. Boats heading to Mangrove Bight can easily drop visitors off at Dina Beach or Michael's Rock, both superb beaches. Regular boats to Savannah Bight leave Guanaja Town daily at 7 A.M., returning immediately, for US$5. An express boat trip to Michael's Rock or elsewhere on the north side costs about US$35–40 each way, depending on gas prices and your negotiating skills.

It's possible to walk the main island's one road from Mangrove Bight, past Mitch, to Savannah Bight, in about an hour.

# Cayos Cochinos (Hog Islands)

The Hog Islands, called the Masaqueras by the early colonists, consist of two main islands and 13 small cays surrounded by pristine reef, 19 kilometers off the Honduran coast. The two larger islands are covered with thick tropical forest and ringed by excellent white-sand beaches. All in all, the Cayos are one of the most spectacular collections of islands, beach, and reef in the western Caribbean, yet they are infrequently visited by most tourists, who instead fly or boat right past on their way to Roatán and Utila.

The Cayos were declared a marine reserve in 1994. All marine and terrestrial flora and fauna within a 460-square-kilometer area is protected from fishing, development, or any other harmful activity. From any point of land in the islands, the reserve extends eight kilometers in all directions. The cays are managed by the **Honduras Coral Reef Fund** (www.cayoscochinos.org), which has a

research center on Cayo Menor. Volunteers are welcome—those interested should send a résumé and cover letter to the HCRF director, Adrian Oviedo, at aeoviedo@cayoscochinos .org. Visitors are charged a US$10 fee for a day visit to the islands, or US$5 if arriving with a tour operator (which may or may not be included in your tour price).

The islands are all privately owned, except for Chachahuate, which holds a small community of a couple of dozen Garífuna families who survive by fishing.

Rides to Cayos Cochinos are available with Javier Arzú in Nueva Armenia, who goes back and forth daily, charging US$13 per person each direction. Call him at 504/9790-9838 the night before to confirm what time to show up, or talk to his sister Alba at 504/9950-5214. Day trips to the Cayos Cochinos can also be arranged from Roatán and Utila, and sailboats can be chartered from Utila for trips of 2–3 days.

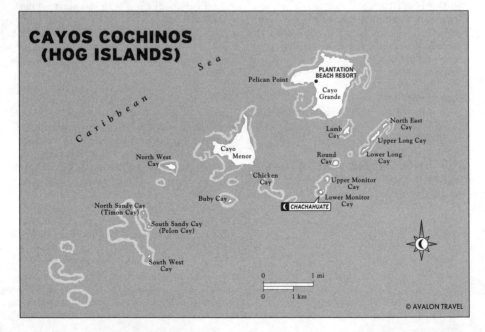

© PETER SVANBERG

Snorkeling is a popular activity on the tiny islands of the Cayos Cochinos.

## **◖ CHACHAHUATE**

Those who wish to appreciate a different side of the Cayos for considerably less money can take a boat from Nuevo Armenia, near Jutiapa on the mainland coast, or from Sambo Creek near La Ceiba, to the Garífuna village of Chachahuate on Lower Monitor Cay. This is the sort of place, as one visitor commented, where you should go with an open mind and heart. Because of its isolation, Chachahuate is one of the more traditional and friendly Garífuna villages in Honduras, so keep that in mind and try to be a relaxed and amiable guest.

An effort is being made to develop ecotourism on the island, and there are now rooms and organized meal service available through the group **Ruta Garinagu Cayos Cochinos.** The mainland coordinator, Chichi, can arrange transportation from Nueva Armenia to Chachahuate (US$130 for round-trip in one day, US$160 for round-trip with a stay of 2–3 days—per boat, not per person), as well as make sure that there are meals and rooms available during your stay. Chichi can be reached at tel. 504/9840-8617 or 504/9937-1702, or

you can stop into **Hotel Chichi** in Nueva Armenia and ask for her. A room in the basic Hotel Chichi is US$5.25 per person, as are the rooms in the simple cabins on Chachahuate (no hot water, and the bathrooms are public baths outside the cabins). In addition to the cabins, there is one hotel, **El Pescador,** which Chichi can also reserve, for US$8 per person. Meals typically consist of a plate of fried fish with rice, beans, and plantain, or *machuca,* a fish soup with plantain. Those who have stayed gave glowing reports about the experience.

Large groups can ask Chichi about the privately owned cay with a guesthouse. Each room in the guesthouse sleeps up to 10.

## **OTHER CAYS**

**Plantation Beach Resort** (tel. 504/442-0974, U.S. tel. 800/346-6116, www.plantation beachresort.com, US$957 pp/week for divers, US$806 pp/week for nondivers) is located on the privately owned Cayo Grande. The hotel's mahogany and stone cottages with decks and hammocks are tucked into a small valley on the site of a former pineapple plantation. PADI

## SWAN ISLANDS

Three days by boat from Guanaja or Puerto Lempira are the tiny Islas del Cisne, the northernmost possession of Honduras in the Caribbean and an extension of the same geological formation that forms the Bay Islands. The Swan Islands lie some 160 kilometers from the Honduran coast. It is said that Columbus landed on the islands in 1502, four days before arriving at Guanaja, and named them the Santa Anas as it was her feast day. The islands are a good source of fresh water, and were frequently used as a way station by Caribbean voyagers over the centuries, and as a result, their ownership has long been disputed. In 1863 the United States decided to take possession under the Guano Islands Act of August 18, 1856, an act that claimed the right to uninhabited and un-owned islands that had plenty of guano – bird dung – for processing as fertilizer. Honduras's claim was made in the 1960s, based on Columbus's stopover on the island, which in their eyes made the islands part of the Spanish colonial empire to which Honduras was the rightful heir. The United States ceded ownership of the Swan Islands to Honduras in 1972 but continued to maintain a radio station there until 1961, reputedly run by the CIA for broadcasting anti-Castro messages in Cuba. The CIA is also rumored to have used the islands as a base for training Nicaraguan Contras.

The Swan Islands – Great Swan, Little Swan, and Booby Cay – can be reached by private boat, helicopter, or plane (there is a small landing strip).

---

certification courses are available. Those looking for some hiking to complement their diving will find numerous trails over the 140-meter peak or around the shore to the north side, where there is a lighthouse and a small village. Rates include all meals, the use of kayaks and snorkel equipment, and, for divers, three boat dives a day, unlimited shore diving, tanks, weights, and belts. Nightly rates are US$116 per person, US$20 more for divers, and the resort accepts cash, travelers checks, or Visa.

The dive shop **Dive in Caribik,** based at the Hotel Palma Real, has also opened up business on one of the smaller cays, "Isla Paradiso," and built the **Eurohonduras Guest House** (tel. 504/3373-8620, www.dive-in-caribik.com, US$80 pp/night, including breakfast, lunch, and dinner). The hotel can also arrange transportation to the tiny island from La Ceiba for another US$60–80, making it logical to spend at least a couple of nights on your own piece of paradise.

## SNORKELING

There's great snorkeling all around, but visitors should bring their own gear, as well as fresh drinking water and a few other supplies like fruit or crackers. Prices vary, but usually a boat from Nuevo Armenia or Sambo Creek should do the trip for US$150–200 (per boat, not per person), or less, depending on your negotiating skills and perceived financial status.

A variety of one-day cruises to the Cayos Cochinos, normally visiting Chachahuate with stops for snorkeling, can be arranged in Roatán and Utila, often for around US$50–70 per person, depending on how many people go; it's extra to bring scuba gear along. It's also possible to arrange trips with one of the tour companies in La Ceiba.

**MOON HONDURAS BAY ISLANDS**
Avalon Travel
a member of the Perseus Books Group
1700 Fourth Street
Berkeley, CA 94710, USA
www.moon.com

Editor and Series Manager: Kathryn Ettinger
Copy Editor: Deana Shields
Graphics Coordinator: Kathryn Osgood
Production Coordinator: Darren Alessi
Cover Designer: Kathryn Osgood
Map Editor: Albert Angulo
Cartographers: Chris Markiewicz, Kat Bennett

ISBN: 978-1-59880-412-6

Text © 2009 by Chris Humphrey and
Amy E. Robertson.

Maps © 2009 by Avalon Travel.
All rights reserved.

Front cover photo: bay island © Peter Svanberg
Title page photo: © Andrea Renda

Printed in in the United States by Edwards Brothers

# ABOUT THE AUTHORS

© NICOLAS OBERPARLEITER

## Chris Humphrey

Chris Humphrey first became smitten by Honduras in 1990 while backpacking through South America. Sitting on a dock in La Ceiba looking to catch a tramp freighter to Nicaragua, he instead hopped a boat out to Utila, in the Bay Islands. Seduced by the mellow Honduran vibe, he wandered on to the soporific beach town of Trujillo and then headed up into the mountains of Olancho, drinking endless cups of wickedly strong coffee and chatting with the local cowboys.

Chris began traveling at the tender age of five, when he ventured across town to a friend's grandmother's house. When he took a year off from college to backpack through Africa and the Middle East, his parents saw the writing on the wall and gave up all efforts to worry about him.

Chris got started as a writer in 1994, after college, when he threw everything into a VW van and moved to Mexico City to work as a journalist. He first wrote for a couple of English-language newspapers, then for a financial wire service, and later as a freelance reporter for whomever deigned to buy his stories, including the *San Francisco Chronicle, National Geographic Traveler, Outside,* and *Latin Finance,* among many others. In 1997, he wrote the first edition of *Moon Honduras.* Chris is also the author of *Moon Mexico City.*

These days, Chris lives in London, England, working on his PhD and wistfully dreaming about sunny beaches, palm trees, and a cold bottle of Salva Vida.

© LUCA RENDA

## Amy E. Robertson

Amy E. Robertson is a Seattle native who has long been obsessed with travel. She studied in Boston and Madrid for her bachelor's degree, and upon graduating took a job with an international consulting firm. This position led Amy to a life of globetrotting – she traveled to more than 50 countries in less than three years. She then returned to school, earning a master's degree in development studies at the London School of Economics, where she also met her husband, who hails from Italy. After working in international aid for five years in New York City, Amy began life as an expat in Ecuador, brought there by her husband's job with the United Nations. Amy made the career switch from development to travel writing while in Ecuador, a livelihood that was easy to bring along when they made the move to Honduras in 2007. Her writing has been published in *National Geographic Traveler, Christian Science Monitor* and *Travel + Leisure,* among others.

Amy currently resides in Tegucigalpa with her husband and two young children, but spends three months a year divided between her family's hometowns: Seattle, Rome, and Messina, Sicily. Together, Amy and her family enjoy exploring the mountain villages, Mayan ruins, white-sand beaches, and lush forests of Central America. Hiking with her kids in Honduras's jungles and cloud forests and spotting birds and crocodiles on the Mosquito Coast are among her favorite experiences.